HowExpert Guide to Collectibles

101+ Tips to Find, Buy, Sell, and Collect Collectibles

HowExpert with Charlotte Hopkins

Copyright HowExpert™
www.HowExpert.com

For more tips related to this topic, visit HowExpert.com/collectibles.

Recommended Resources

- HowExpert.com – Quick 'How To' Guides on All Topics from A to Z by Everyday Experts.
- HowExpert.com/free – Free HowExpert Email Newsletter.
- HowExpert.com/books – HowExpert Books
- HowExpert.com/courses – HowExpert Courses
- HowExpert.com/clothing – HowExpert Clothing
- HowExpert.com/membership – HowExpert Membership Site
- HowExpert.com/affiliates – HowExpert Affiliate Program
- HowExpert.com/writers – Write About Your #1 Passion/Knowledge/Expertise & Become a HowExpert Author.
- HowExpert.com/resources – Additional HowExpert Recommended Resources
- YouTube.com/HowExpert – Subscribe to HowExpert YouTube.
- Instagram.com/HowExpert – Follow HowExpert on Instagram.
- Facebook.com/HowExpert – Follow HowExpert on Facebook.

Publisher's Foreword

Dear HowExpert Reader,

HowExpert publishes quick 'how to' guides on all topics from A to Z by everyday experts.

At HowExpert, our mission is to discover, empower, and maximize talents of everyday people to ultimately make a positive impact in the world for all topics from A to Z...one everyday expert at a time!

All of our HowExpert guides are written by everyday people just like you and me who have a passion, knowledge, and expertise for a specific topic.

We take great pride in selecting everyday experts who have a passion, great writing skills, and knowledge about a topic that they love to be able to teach you about the topic you are also passionate about and eager to learn about.

We hope you get a lot of value from our HowExpert guides and it can make a positive impact in your life in some kind of way. All of our readers including you altogether help us continue living our mission of making a positive impact in the world for all spheres of influences from A to Z.

If you enjoyed one of our HowExpert guides, then please take a moment to send us your feedback from wherever you got this book.

Thank you and we wish you all the best in all aspects of life

Sincerely,

BJ Min
Founder & Publisher of HowExpert
HowExpert.com

PS...If you are also interested in becoming a HowExpert author, then please visit our website at HowExpert.com/writers. Thank you & again, all the best!

Table of Contents

Chapter 1: How to Start and Grow A Collection

- How to Choose the Best Collectible for You

- Collectible Terms You Should Know

- Keeping Good Records and Notes

- Collectible Books and Newspapers

- Origin of Collectibles and Many Firsts

Getting Started with Collectibles

Welcome to the world of SuperCollectors! This is where one is a treasured find - two is a set - and three makes a collection. Sometimes a collection gets started when a person is given a gift, or they inherit an item, and these hold such sentimental value that we have a desire to add more. Then there are collectors who come across an object that grabs their attention and sparks a desire to find more and more! There may also be a time when we spot an item that is exactly what we had as a child or something that looks like an item a grandparent owned. The object triggers memories that we want to hold on to – and a collection is grown from there.

Tip 1: Where to Start

There are several ways to get started in learning about antiques. One way is to visit antique stores and fellow collectors. They love to talk about their treasured finds and to educate the public. An auction house and an antique fair are other ways to learn. They have studied the history of their pieces and include the information in their brochures and programs. These are more places where you can search for collectibles.

The website Antique Trader is chock full of information about collectibles. Along with discussing the different collectibles, they delve into the history and value of the items. You can also find information about antique shops, museums, and stories about collectors and their experiences.

The website, Replacements.com, will come in handy if your collection is a piece of a set. The site can help you find different pieces to complete your collection. There are also cleaning materials, storage items, and items needed to display your items. You can even shop for ornaments, figurines, village houses, and more.

You will read several times in this book the importance of knowing the history of collectibles. Homes & Antiques is a phenomenal website that explores the history of many collectibles throughout the years. They also give tips on displaying your pieces.

Tip 2: What to Consider When Starting a Collection

When choosing a collectible, there are several factors to consider. Do you have the room for your collectible? Salt & Pepper shakers, egg plates, or mustache cups will fill shelves nicely. Still, others need a wider set of shelves and, eventually, their own room. Do you have a favorite animal? Sport or team? Hobby? Is there something about your profession that you adore enough to want to make into a collection? For example, police officers & firefighters collect patches, and accountants collect calculators. And remember, there is no rule that says you cannot have more than one collection. Some choose a collectible based on the value, and if they can sell it in the future for a higher cost.

Whether you are a collector as an investor or want to save items that you cherish, be sure to learn the history of your collectible. This will widen your scope of knowledge, helping you age your treasured finds, which will also help you determine its value. It will also keep you from being conned by people who try to sell an item to you at a higher cost, claiming it is an antique. Here are a few examples. Automobiles did not have speedometers until 1901, and the Olds Motor Vehicle Company started it. Harley-Davidson did not make their gas tanks in a teardrop shape until 1925. Zip codes were first used in 1963. The first cash register was built in 1879 by John Ritty. There are several category collectibles.

Tip 3: Online Courses for Collectors

The website Learningwithexperts.com offers several online courses under a variety of subjects dealing with antiques and collectibles.

The two websites Universal Class (universalclass.com) and Udemy (udemy.com) offer courses on buying and selling antiques & collectibles. At Udemy, there are also courses on how to collect books and an introduction to stamp collecting. There is also a course on how to "Find, Fix, and Sell Vintage Tonka Trucks."

The Asheford Institute of Antiques (asheford.com) is an online school dedicated to everything related to antiques and collectibles.

Tip 4: Antiques vs. Collectibles vs. Vintage

Though some people can collect antiques, not all collectibles are antiques. It is simple to remember. An antique is an item that is more than 100 years old. A collectible is anything new, and up to 100 years old. Then you have vintage collectibles. "Vintage" describes any item that is between 20 - 99 years old.

Tip 5: Different Terms Collectors

Should Know

Amboyna – This is a reddish-brown type of wood from Indonesia.

Arcading – A design in the shape of an arch, found on chair-backs and coffers.

Cased Glass – This is what they call layers of blown glass.

Chinoiserie – In the 16th century, the Portuguese had ceramics imported into the United States. They referred to them as Chinoiserie. It also describes collectibles that have an Asian look.

Coin Silver – A piece that is 90% silver.

Conservator – A person who repairs and preserves collectibles and antiques.

Cordwainer – This is a person who made shoes.

Crizzling (or Weeping Glass) – This happens when there is an instability of the glass during production that gives it either a look of tiny cracks or a cloudy appearance.

Curio - A term referred to a curious and intriguing item.

Diaperwork – A repeating pattern of diamond shapes.

EPNS – These are initials that stand for Electro-Plated Nickel Silver. This is used to make cutlery that will last for generations.

Foxing – A type of mold that appears as brown dots on vintage ephemera that has not been stored properly. This happens mostly on maps.

Garage Kit – A model kit using figures made of resin.

Heirloom – This describes an object that has belonged to the same family for several generations.

Kitsch – This is a name given to ugly collectibles. Yes, these are items actually made to look ugly.

Manufactured Collectible (Contemporary Collectible) – This is an item that was made to be collected. These are items marked "Limited Edition" and "Special Edition.

Mint – Item is still in the original condition with the original packaging.

Mocha – This describes an artistic and swirl design found on ceramics.

Patina – Everything that happens to an item over a period of time. This includes dusting, polishing, neglect, sun damage, scratches, dings, and sagging.

Preambulator - This was once the name for baby carriages.

Repro – An new item that is created to look like an antique.

Soakies – A collector of bubble bath bottles gave his collection this name. It stuck on, and now collectors of plastic figure bubble bath containers call them "soakies."

Tapestry – A heavy fabric that is hand-woven and used on the back of chairs.

Tip 6: Keep Good Records

Collectors should keep track of each item in their collection. This record is called a provenance. Remember that word. It will come up again when someone asks to see your provenance. This is a detailed record that collectors maintain for each piece they own. The first thing you need to do is assign a number to the item. In your notes, write the name of the object with the corresponding number along with a description. Note when and where you bought the piece or if it was given to you. Were there any appraisals or restorations done to the piece. If so, when did it occur and who did the work. Save certificates and photos of each collectible. Save checks and receipts with it. Be sure to copy the designated number onto the picture, if possible. Then write the number on each document that goes with the collectible piece. Save the information in a notebook or a 3-ring binder. If you use the binder, store the photos and paperwork in sheet protectors. Do not poke holes in them. Any auction house or antique dealer will tell you the extreme importance of provenance.

Tip 7: Companies Behind Collectibles and Antiques

Collectors of dishes, figurines, and housewares tend to focus on a favored style or company. These are some of the companies admired by collectors. When researching the name of the company that produced your piece, you will want to note these details of their history.

Name Changes

Who founded the company?

First year of business

Where were they located, if they moved, learn their different locations, and when they were there?

What are all of the items they produced (these changes through time)?

Last year of production (if it applies), and the location(s) of the company – from start to finish.

Royal Doulton	Kemple Glass
Glass Baron	Liberty Blue Design
Mary Engelbreit	Lenox
FJ Designs	Fenton Glass
Sandicast	Atterbury

Department 56	Emmett Kelly JR
Bradford Exchange	Nipon
Hagen-Renake	Occupied Japan
Heisey Glass	England

Tip 8: Basic Rules to Obtaining Autographs for Collections

When getting your collectibles signed, there are two things to remember. If it is on fabric, then it should be signed with a Sharpie. Balls, from any sport, should be signed with a ballpoint pen. When you save an autographed collectible, make sure the autograph is clear or crisp. The condition of the item itself is also important. There should be no damage, smudges, creases, or smears. Timing is also crucial. Did you receive the autograph before their death? Was it at the beginning or end of an event, such as war or change in career?

Tip 9: Facts about Collectible Figurines

In the world of collectible figurines, there is a wide variety. That selection includes Willow Tree, Kelvin's, Hanford, Hummel, Erich Stauffer, and Napco Figurines. That is just to name a few. There are many more you can discover on your journey.

Lladro was founded by brothers, Juán, José and Vicente Lladro, in1953. They first made vases and jugs. They started making figurines in 1956.

Precious Moments was introduced in 1975 on inspirational cards and posters. The figurines were introduced in 1978.

Cherished Teddies, made by ENESCO, are the most sought after figurines of teddy bears. They were created from the drawings of Priscilla Hillman and her son Glenn Herman. They were first sold in 1992.

Paula Figurines are whimsical "trophies" from the 1970s that acknowledged things like the best mom, a wonderful bowler or just had a fun message depicted on the trophy. They were made by PAULA, a section of the Wallace Berrie Company.

When Snowbabies were introduced in 1986 by Department 56, they were known as "sugar babies." They were made out of sugar and used for cake decorations. Germany started making them out of porcelain. Other countries began making them out of chalkware because they didn't want to buy from Germany during Hitler's domain. The older figurines are referred to as "Oldbabies."

Tip 10: What to Know about Collectible Books

Book collectors mostly focus on a specific author or genre. There are also book collectors that search for miniatures, First Editions, and Little Golden Books. When judging the value of books, the condition is critical when determining value. These are the grades" that are used when determining the condition of a book.

Very Fine (VF) - A flawless book, the closest to being brand new.

Fine (F) – These books may have one or two small bumps. They are also known as "carefully read." The dust jacket should be undamaged.

Near Fine (NF) – This has some wear & tear, and one or two small flaws.

Very Good (VG) – Several minor flaws, nothing major.

Good (G) – A typical used book can have minor and major flaws.

Fair (FR) – Worn condition, loose binding, minor and major flaws, known as well-read. The dust jacket is missing, along with one or more mom-essential pages.

Poor (P) – Very bad condition, considered acceptable for reading but not collecting.

Dame Juliana Berners wrote "A Treatyse of Fysshynge wyth an Angle," in 1496. This was the first book about the proper way to fish

Samuel Richardson wrote, "Pamela," in 1740. This was the first romance novel.

Edgar Allen Poe wrote "The Murder in the Rue Morgue" in 1841. This is the first modern detective story.

In 1859, Wilkie Collins wrote "Woman in White." This is considered the first mystery novel.

The first phone book was published on July 2, 1874.

Fannie Farmer published the Boston Cooking-School Cookbook in 1896. In that book, she introduced the concept of using measuring spoons and measuring cups. She also created the format for the modern recipe, which lists the ingredients first, precise measurements, and the directions listed in order.

Tip 11: Collectible CliffNotes

Some of us would never have made it through the literary classics without the help of Clifton Hillegass. He is the "Cliff" behind CliffsNotes, those little yellow study guides that condense a hundred pages of Shakespeare into three concise paragraphs. Each volume of his study guides included a signed note to his readers: "A thorough appreciation of literature allows no shortcuts." Hillegass started his company with a $4,000 loan in 1958 and published 16 Shakespearean study guides. He ran his company from the basement of his Lincoln, Nebraska home. His wife and daughter helped by stuffing envelopes and mailing letters to contacts.

When he found out that students were using them as chest guides, he added this disclaimer to his books: "These notes are not a substitute for the text itself or for the classroom discussion of the text, and students who attempt to use them in this way are denying themselves the very education that they are presumably giving their most vital years to achieve."

When the company started, the name of the books was "Cliff's Notes." In 1964, they dropped the apostrophe from their name and became "Cliffs Notes." In 1998, he sold Cliffs Notes to IDG Books for $14 million. The name was changed once more in 2001 when they were bought by John Wiley & Sons. The name changed to "CliffsNotes." Cliff passed away in 2001, but his memory lives on in his native Nebraska. For 40 years, he donated 10% of his profits to local charitable causes.

Tip 12: Book Firsts

William Shakespeare created the name "Jessica." When J.M. Barrie wrote "Peter Pan," he created the name "Wendy."

William Shakespeare created words and expressions that we still use today. And like Shakespeare, Dr. Seuss often created his own words when he could not find just the right one to use. This was the case in 1950, when he created the word "nerd" for his book, "If I Ran the Zoo."

"French author, Charles Perot, wrote "Cendrillon" in 1697. Walt Disney rewrote it as his version "Cinderella." It is noted that Perot's "Cendrillon" is the first fairy tale.

Another notable book by Dr. Seuss is The Lorax. This was his nod to environmentalism and how destructive humans are treating the planet, Earth. A few felt the book made them look bad; the logging industry was one of them. In turn, they wrote The Truax, which was an attempt to tell their side of the issue. The book also has the line, "I hear things are just as bad up in Lake Erie." This caught the eye of Ohio residents. Fourteen years later, the Ohio Sea Grant Program reached out to Dr. Seauss, informing him that Lake Erie's conditions have greatly improved. They asked him to please remove the line from his book. He graciously agreed that it would no longer be included in future editions.

Tip 13: Newspaper Dates Collectors Should Know

It is impossible to have copies of the first newspapers published, but as mentioned previously, it is essential to know the history of collectibles. Here is a timeline through the stages of the newspaper field.

59 BC: Acta Diurna, the first newspaper, is published in Rome.

1556: First monthly newspaper, the "Notizie Scritte," is published in Venice.

1605: First weekly newspaper, titled "Relation," is published in Antwerp (Belgium).

1690: "Publick Occurrence," America's first newspaper is published.

1702: The "Daily Courant" was the first English language daily newspaper. It was first printed in 1621.

1704: Daniel Defoe publishes the Review. He is considered the world's first journalist. Also, that year on May 8, 1704, the Boston News-Letter published the first ad. It was for the sale of property on Oyster Bay, Long Island.

1831: The famous abolitionist newspaper, The Liberator, is first published by William Lloyd Garrison.

1833: The New York Sun newspaper costs one cent - the beginning of the penny press.

1851: The Post Office starts offering a special cheap newspaper rate.

1856: The first full-page newspaper ad is published in the New York Ledger. Large type newspaper ads are made famous by photographer Mathew Brady. Machines now mechanically fold newspapers.

1860: A "morgue" in newspaper terms means an archive. The New York Herald starts the first morgue.

1864: William James Carlton of J. Walter Thompson Company begins selling advertising space in newspapers. Today, the J. Walter Thompson Company is the longest-running American advertising agency.

1873: First illustrated daily newspaper published in New York.

1877: First weather report with a map published in Australia. The Washington Post newspaper first publishes with a circulation of 10,000 and a cost of 3 cents per paper.

1903: The first tabloid-style newspaper, the Daily Mirror, is published.

Tip 14: How to Spot a "First"

J. Roderick MacArthur founded the Bradford Exchange in 1973. They are most known for their porcelain dolls. Their first porcelain doll was "Jason," and it sold for $48.

Collectible plates got their start in Denmark in the 1800s. They were wooden and wealthy landowners gave them as Christmas gifts to the families who lived and worked on their land. They would gift them with baked goods, and when they were done with the treats, they saved the plates. When the cost of porcelain dropped, they used porcelain plates instead of wooden. The first porcelain plates were blue and white and had a Christmas design. In 1895, Bing & Grondahl made the plate, "Behind the Frozen Window." This was the world's first true collector's plate.

If you come across a calculator that bears the name ANITA, those were the first calculators and were introduced in 1956. They were on a larger scale, so they were desktop. Texas Instruments debuted in 1967. They made the first handheld calculators. One of their original calculators is on display at the Smithsonian.

The Lenox Company was founded by Walter Scott Lenox and opened in 1889. They were the first makers of the china used in the White House. Their work was inducted into the Smithsonian Institution in 1897.

The most famous rifle in American history was created in Lancaster County, Pennsylvania, during the min1700s. It was named the Pennsylvania Long Rifle. This set the stage for rifles to come.

Tip 15: Accidental Collectible

Though there have been mistakes on collectibles that made them more valuable, there are also accidents that become collectibles. Here are some accidental collectibles. Take note of the years these things happened.

In 1904, tea bags were invented accidentally. Thomas Sullivan decided it was cheaper to send small samples to potential customers in silk bags instead of boxes of loose tea. The recipients thought they were supposed to dunk the bag in hot water. Sullivan was soon flooded with orders for his "tea bags."

Harry Brearley attempted to make a new type of metal for guns stronger than iron. He examined the metal he created but found no use for it. So, Brearley put it aside. Months later, in 1913, while looking through the scrap he had thrown out, he realized that one of the discarded pieces had not rusted. By accident, he discovered stainless steel.

People originally used bread to erase pencil marks. In 1770, Edward Naine picked up a piece of rubber instead of bread and found it to be effective. He then started to sell rubber erasers. So, the item created to fix mistakes was invented because of a mistake.

Though many items made their first debut at the World's Fair, we can credit the St. Louis World's Fair of 1904 with another accidental invention. It stemmed more out of necessity. Ernest A. Hamwi was selling waffle-like desserts next to a man selling ice cream. When he ran out of cups, Hamwi stepped in to help. He rolled one of his waffles into the shape of a cornucopia. This was the first waffle cone. Though Italy invented the first ice cream cone, credit for the waffle cone goes to Hamwi.

Tip 16: Popular (and valuable) Collectibles Today

What is popular among collectibles changes by the decade. It is hard to tell which one of today's items will soar in value. These are some of today's most valuable collectibles.

Birkin bags	Soda Crates
Costume Jewelry	Art Deco Clocks
Stetson Hats	Photographs
Purses (from the 50s - 70s)	Typewriters
Jewelry Presentation Box	Vinyl Records
Chinoiserie	Advertising Signs
Jadeite Pieces	Lunch Boxes
Christmas Decorations	Cast Iron Mailboxes
Royal Daulton and Royal Worcester	Mechanical Banks
Duck Decoys	Victor Radios and Record Players
Football Programs	Space Memorabilia
Movie and Concert Posters	Boy Scouts Memorabilia
VHS Tapes	Super Bowl Memorabilia
Belly Boards	Women's Suffrage Memorabilia
Guitars	Campaign Memorabilia
Tools	Silver Cups
Postcards	Trunks

Tip 17: What Type of Collector are You?

These terms describe specific types of Collectors. You will hear them mentioned at auction houses, conventions, and antique shops.

Aerophilately – A person that collects items relating to airmail.

Aichmomania – A collector of knives, swords, and similar sharp items.

Arctophilist - A person who collects teddy bears.

Arenophile – This is a person who collects sand samples from around the world.

Bibliophilist – A person who collects books. Some look for specific types such as Little Golden books, antique books, miniatures, First Editions, a favorite author, or genre.

Brandophilist – A person who collects cigar bands.

Breweriana – Alcohol-related Items. Some contain a brewery or brand name. These items include shot glasses, beer bottles, and cans, glasses, coasters, advertising materials.

Labeorphilist - This is a collector of beer bottles.

Labologist – Someone who collects beer bottle labels.

Cagophily – Someone who specializes in the collection of keys.

Cartophilist – A collector of cigarette cards and trading cards. The most popular trading cards are baseball cards. Cigarette cards came inside the packs of cigarettes between 1875 to the 1940s. They were fun for the customers, but for the manufacturers, they were used to stiffen the package to protect the cigarettes from being damaged.

Conchologist – Someone who collects seashells.

Copoclephilist – A collector of Key Rings (keychains).

Deltiologist - A person who concentrates on collecting postcards.

Digitabulist – A person who collects thimbles.

Discophile - A person who collects both phonographs and CDs.

Ephemera – A collection of items made from paper, such as paper dolls, paper dresses, food labels, magazines, newspapers, and envelopes. These items were not meant to last.

Falerist – Someone who collects medals, badges, pins, and other military and civilian awards and decorations.

Fusilatelist – Someone who collects phone cards.

Grabatologist – A person who collects ties.

Helixophile – A person who collects corkscrews.

Juvenilia – A collector who looks for toys, dolls, dollhouses, toy soldiers, trains, teddy bears, and games.

Lepidopterist – A person who studies or collects butterflies and moths.

Lincolniana – A collection of Abraham Lincoln memorabilia.

Lotologist – A person who collects lottery tickets and lottery memorabilia.

Memomagnetist - A person who collects kitchen magnets.

Militaria – A collection of military-related artifacts and memorabilia.

Notaphilist - This is someone who solely collects paper money.

Numismatist – A person who collects coins, tokens, paper money, and medals.

Pannapictagraphist – Someone who collects comic books.

Pharologist – A person who collects Lighthouse memorabilia.

Philatelist – A person who collects stamps and postal items.

Phillumenist - A collector of matchbooks, matchboxes, matchbox labels, and match items.

Philographist – Someone who specializes in collecting autographs.

Phonophily – This is the collection of phonographs.

Plangonologist - A person who collects dolls.

Pucillovist – A collector of Egg Cups.

Scripophilist – A collector of old bonds and certificates.

Scutelliphily – The hobby of collecting all types of patches. They sometimes refer to the patches as "badges."

Sucrology - is the hobby of collecting sugar packets, including wrappers, sachets, tubes, sticks, packs, bags, and squares.

Tegestologist – This is someone who collects coasters (also called beer mats).

Tobacciana – Collectibles of tobacco products, including ashtrays, lighters, matchbooks, cigars, cigarettes, pipes, tobacco tins, and items relating to smoking.

Toxophilist – A collector of bows and arrows.

Tyrosemiophile This is someone who specializes in the collection of cheese labels.

Vecturist - A collector of automobile tokens.

Vexillophile – A person who studies and collects flags.

Chapter 2: Know the Details

- Labels and Addresses

- Collectible Firsts

- Logos, Markings, and Symbols

- Details that Age Your Collectibles

- Details on Furniture Legs

Know the Details

One way to learn the authenticity and age of your collectibles is to recognize different details, logos, and names. For example, an item with whiskey, spelled with the "e" comes from Ireland. An item with "whisky" spelled without the "e" comes from Scotland or Canada. While you search for collectibles to add to your collections, you may meet people that try to pass objects off for being older than they actually are. Details on the label indicate the age of your collectibles and if it is authentic. Here are some features to look for on your labels.

Tip 18: Who Said That?

An interesting part of an item's history is "who named it." This is the origin of everyday words to everyday collectibles.

In 1899, the New York Times coined the word "automobile" in an article about the new horseless-carriage.

"Good to the Last Drop" is a slogan used by Maxwell House since 1915. It was first used by Coca-Cola in 1908.

The expression, "Loose Lips Sink Ships" was first used as a WWII slogan.

William Whewell coined the word "scientist" in 1833.

The word "millionaire" was first used in the novel, "Vivian Grey," by Benjamin Disraeli.

Charles Boycott was a Land Agent who lived from 1932-1897. People so hated him that after his death, his name became a verb.

The first restaurant was built in Paris in 1765. Their main dish was bowls of broths. Their first (and only) food dish was sheep's feet in white sauce. Restaurer, means "to restore" in French. That is what was used to derive the word "restaurant."

Tip 19: Collectible Firsts

These are random "first facts" that will help you later when you are dating your collectibles and antiques.

Matches were created by John Walker in 1827.

In 1736, New Amsterdam, Philadelphia, became the home of the first fire department in America. It was organized by Ben Franklin. He originally called the firefighters "prowlers."

Queen Victoria's husband, Prince Albert, introduced Christmas trees to England in 1841.

John Joseph Merlin designed the first pair of roller skates in 1760. James Plimpton improved on his invention in 1858.

William Austin Burt invented the typographer in 1829, the predecessor to the typewriter.

Christopher Sholes created the modern typewriter on June 23, 1868.

The modern thermos was created in 1907 by the American Thermos Bottle Company.

Bubble Gum is different than chewing gum. It is a stronger gum that comes in a wider variety of flavors. It was introduced in 1928 by the Fleer Company. Bubble Gum is pink because it was the only color the inventor had left.

Jann Wennerm, a UC Berkley dropout, started Rolling Stone magazine in 1867 with money he borrowed from his girlfriend's parents.

Seymour, Washington is the home of the original hamburger, In 1885, Charles, the Hamburger, Nagreen, 15 years old, made them at the local fair.

Peter Heinlein created the first watch in 1724

The first $1 bill was issued in 1862 and had "Salmon P. Chase pictured on it – He was the secretary of treasury – in 1869 – they started using the portrait of George Washington painted by Gilbert Stuart.

Tip 20: Definitions of Markings

The letters, words, and symbols on the items that are used to identify the product are called "Maker's marks" or "Identifiers." These are some of the more specific marks.

Incised Mark – These are marks applied to the pottery by hand after the item is made and before the first firing.

Impressed Mark – These marks are also applied when the item is finished and before the first firing, but they are stamped on instead of carved.

Underglaze Marks – Markings added after the firing but before the glaze is applied.

Overglaze Marks – These markings are applied after the glaze firing and before the final firing.

Pressed Back – Pieces that have designs that were stamped or pressed into the wood.

Qianlong Marks – These are marks found on Chinese porcelain pieces. They detail the dynasty and reign during the production of the item.

Tip 21: A History of Glassware Marks

Glass Lovers Glass Database is a go-to site for all types of glass collectors. Through the website, collectors can identify the makers, the eras, most importantly, the markings on the glass. With these items being produced for several centuries, there are dozens and dozens of markings that tell the history of each piece. All of that information can be found on this website. The item numbers, marks, and logos are the language of glass. If the information about your piece does not appear on the item, the team at Glass Lovers Glass Database can help you find it.

Tip 22: What is in the Name

The first step to identifying collectibles is to research identifying marks left by the creator or manufacturer. These marks will uncover the rich and detailed history of the object.

Marks on jewelry are small; you may need a magnifying glass to find them. These marks are also known as identifiers. For rings, they are found inside. For watches, brooches, and pendants, they are located on the underside. For earrings, they are on the posts. For necklaces and bracelets, they can be found on the clasp.

The first step that details the purity of the piece is called "Hallmarks." Gold jewelry is made using the karat system, which includes 24 karats. It is marked with a number and a "k." So if all parts are gold, it will say "24K." If only 14 parts are gold, then it will say "14K." Silver is marked "sterling" or with the numbers "925." Platinum will be marked "PT" or "PLAT."

There are more markings on jewelry that include the following.

CT - Carat

CTW - Carat total weight

CZ - Cubic zirconia

F - Flawless

I - Included (I1, I2, I2)

IF - Internally flawless

SI - Slightly included (SI1, S12)

TW - Total weight

VSI - Very slightly included (VS1, VS2)

VVSI - Very very slightly included (VVS1, VVS2)

The "Marks Project" website is an excellent resource for searching a variety of markings.

Collectors can contact the National American Glass Club to learn about the markings and history of different glassware products (any type). The club was established in 1933. An example of a glassware label is the "K" for Kemple Glass. They labeled their items simply with a letter K. Their early pieces have a letter K with a circle. During the 1960s, it was a letter K inside a square. More symbols can be found on the website: **glassloversglassdatabase.com**.

Tip 23: Eras and Terms to Age and Classify Collectibles

There are several terms that describe the age of collectibles. They are commonly used when dating jewelry and watches, but they can be used for all items made during that time. Period-Style describes items from a particular era. These are eras used by collectors and antique dealers.

Tudor Era 1485–1603

Elizabethan Era 1558–1603

Baroque period 1600-1750

Jacobean Era 1603-1625

Georgian Era 1714-1837

Industrial Revolution 1760-1840

Federal Era 1788-1800

Regency Era 1811-1820

Gothic Revival 1830-1860

Victorian Era 1837-1901

Renaissance Revival 1860-1875

Edwardian Era 1901-1910

Bauhaus Era 1919-1933

Depression Era 1930-1939

Mid-Century 1933-1965

Danish Modern Era 1940-1970

Atomic Age 1940-1970

Pop Culture 1955-1980

Hippie Movement 1965-1978

Disco Era 1973-1980

Egyptian Revival 1830-1850 & 1870-1900 & 1920-1940

The term "Estate Jewelry" describes any item that was previously owned, regardless of the age. "Trench Art" refers to objects, specifically jewelry, made by soldiers and prisoners of war. These items were first crafted by soldiers when they were in the trenches. They used old utensils to make jewelry to send home. They were pieces like rings made from spoon handles.

Tip 24: Recognize the Name Changes

Many companies that produce some of our favorite collectibles have changed names through the years. When you learn the history behind your collectibles, include the company itself in your studies. Knowing the times of any name changes will, again, help you to age your collectible. For example, did you know that Nintendo manufactured toilet paper before they made video games? Here are examples of companies that changed their names through the years.

Through the years, some companies have changed their names. Learning the company's history will help you date your collectible. For example, the Atterbury Company was established in Pittsburgh, Pennsylvania, from 1860-1902. When they first opened, they were known as Atterbury & Company. A year later (1861), they were re-organized as Atterbury, Reddick & Company. In 1863, they were renamed again to J.S. & T. B. Atterbury. In 1865, they underwent more changes and became Atterbury &

Company. In 1896, they changed their name for the last time to Atterbury Glass Company. They kept that name until 1902. They were also referred to as the White House Factory. They earned this nickname because their factory was painted white, and they produced a line of Milk Glass.

The Royal Doulton Company opened in Lambeth, London, in 1815 and was known as the "Doulton Company." They got their start making bottles and sewer pipes. In 1882, they moved to Nile Street in Burslem. In 1901, they changed their name to "Royal Doulton."

During World War II, the United States banned Japanese items from being shipped in and sold. To sidestep that regulation, they marked their items "Nippon." That means "made in Japan" in Japanese.

In 1964, Bill Bowerman and Phil Knight established Blue Ribbon Sports and created running shoes. They met at the University of Oregon when Knight ran on the track team that was coached by Bowerman. In 1965, they teamed with the Tiger Shoe Company and made running shoes until 1971, when the merger fell apart. Also, that year, Knight and Bowerman redesigned the company and named it Nike. Carolyn Davis, a Design student at Portland State University, created the swoosh design and was paid $35 for it.

Tip 25: What is in Those Numbers

Crocks have a number either 3 or 5 imprinted on either the side or under the handle. The number indicates whether the jar holds 3 or 5 gallons or quarts for smaller crocks.

A regiment is a military unit. The size of the regiment and their role in the military varies by country. The term was first used in Medieval Europe. Military collectibles should have a regiment number on it. If it does not, then it is most likely a reproduction.

A serial number is substantial because it shows the position of an item in a series when it was made. The lower the serial number, the better.

Identifying Numbers are found on antique furniture, usually on the back. The numbers indicate the style, maker, and patent numbers.

Tip 26: What Soft Drink Names Can Tell You

You do not have to be a soft drinker collector to have one, or even a few, among your saved collectibles. Whether it is Barbie dolls, coasters, playing cards, or even thimbles – you will find pieces with soft drinks emblazoned on them. For that reason, collectors should get to know the names, name changes, and history of soft drinks. The more you know about the history of soft drinks, the better educated you are when adding these pieces to your collections.

The first soft drinks were sold in the mid-1600s. It was a concoction of water, lemon juice, and honey. In 1767, Englishman Joseph Priestley discovered a method of making carbonated water by fusing it with carbonated water. This was the beginning of the soft drink craze.

Schweppe's opened in 1783, making it the first and oldest soft drink manufacturer. It was given the name "soft drink" because it did not contain alcohol. The first product sold by Schweppe's was Carbonated Water. Ginger Ale was not invented in Ireland in 1783, and it was still not sold as a soft drink until Vernors released it in 1866. The soft drinks that followed Vernors Ginger Ale were Hires Root Beer (1876), Moxie (1885), Dr. Pepper (1885), Coca Cola (1886), Pepsi (1893), and Barq's Root Beer (1898).

Caleb Davis Bradham developed brad's Drink in 1893. The name was changed to Pepsi Cola in 1898. He believed it to be a health drink that could aid with dyspepsia. Pepsi is the only other soft drink company to use the name Cola other than Coke because they were the only ones to successfully sue Coke over the right to use the name Cola. The judge stated that since Cola is used for the Cola bean that Coke could not claim it as solely their own. Early soft drinks were peddled as medicine for different ailments; this is why they started with names like Root Beer and Ginger Ale.

Another drink that changed its name was 7up. It was initially called Bib-label Lithiated Lemon-Lime Soda. The drink was introduced in October 1929. The name was changed to 7Up in 1936.

Tip 27: Details to Look for in the Address

If there is an address on the label, keep in mind that before 1963, there were no zip codes used on addresses. When people listed the address, they would use the first four letters for the state. For example, Pennsylvania would be "Penn." They noticed that some states with the same first two letters would get their mail mixed up, such as Minneapolis and Mississippi or even the North and South states. To fix the problem, the post office developed a system of using zip codes. This came about in early 1963. However, some states said the line was taking up a lot of space now that they applied the 5-digit zip code. The Post Office went back to work to fix that. In October, they issued a 2-letter abbreviation to each state. Keep in mind, if the state is written in four letters, it was made before 1963. Anything with a zip code was created after October 1963.

The Cloverine Salve is an example of using the address to date the collectible. Cloverine Salve is a patent remedy that was used to treat chapped and dry skin and came in a tin. It was first made during the 1930s, in Tyrone, Pennsylvania. The tins are sought after by collectors, specifically the older ones – the originals. In the 1960s, they moved to New York. They moved once more in the 1970s to Jackson, Wyoming. To determine the original from the newer tins can be found in the address. When the company was located in Tyrone, the state was abbreviated "Penn," and there was no zip code since it was not yet created. When they moved to New York, the zip code was added. So, none of the originals will ever have a zip code.

Tip 28: Recognize Different Label Types

President Lincoln started the Department of Agriculture and the Bureau of Chemistry in 1862. This office was the predecessor of the Food and Drug Administration (FDA). In 1940, they started listing ingredients on the label. Sterilization labels began in 1957. In 1973, the USDA required Nutrition information to be added to labels. That same year, some of the first products ere labeled "organic." This started with the California Certified Organic Farmers.

Tip 29: What is Written on the Bottom?

More clues to your collectibles can be found on the bottom. If there are no markings on the bottom, then the item was made before 1810. Here are some things to look for that will indicate when the piece was made.

"Copyright" was written from 1850-1913.

The © symbol was used after 1924.

"Registered" was written on items from England.

"Depose" means "registered" in French.

After 1910, items were marked, "Made in 'country name.'"

"Made In England" was written on items in 1921.

"Limited" or the abbreviation "Ltd" was used on items made after 1851.

Tip 30: What You Should Know about English Registry Marks

In 1842, England started shipping items that included a design label known as the English Registry Mark. It is filled with information about the object. The Registry Mark is a diamond shape with a circle on top. It also had the letters Rd in the center of the diamond with two lines under the "d." It stands for "registered." Inside the circle is a Roman numeral that describes the material that was used to make the piece.

I – metal

II – wood

III – glass

IV – ceramics

This is the information that explains the details inside the mark 1842-1867. The letter inside the top section shows the year that the item was registered. This chart lists those numerals and matching years.

1842—X	1851—P	1860—Z
1843—H	1852—D	1861—R
1844—C	1853—Y	1862—O
1845—A	1854—J	1863—G
1846—I	1855—E	1864—N
1847—F	1856—L	1865—W
1848—U	1857—K	1866—Q
1849—S	1858—B	1867—T
1850—V	1859—M	

The number on the bottom is the parcel number (a code that represents the person or company that created the item).

The number on the right is the day of the month that the item was registered. The letter on the left indicates the month of the year.

C—January	I—July
G—February	R—August
W—March	D—September
H—April	B—October
E—May	K—November
M—June	A—December

The information inside the diamond was changed and from 1868 – 1883, and it represented the following. The number in the top section stood for the day of the month that the item was registered. The letter on the bottom stands for the month. The letter on the right stands for the year that it was registered. The number on the left is the parcel number.

Tip 31: The Seven Types of Logos

There are seven types of logos: Monogram or Lettermark, Mascot Logo, Emblem Logo, Pictorial Mark or Logo Symbol, Abstract Logo Mark, Wordmark or Logotype, and Combination Mark.

Monogram or Lettermark: Logos that consist only of letters (NASA).

Mascot Logo: A character created to represent a product. (Kool-Aid Pitcher)

Emblem Logo: A symbol that includes a badge, seal, or crest (Harley-Davidson)

Pictorial Mark or Logo Symbol: A brand mark or logo picture that symbolizes a company (Twitter Bird)

Abstract Logo Mark: A type of Pictorial Mark that is made from an abstract shape (Pepsi circle)

Wordmark or Logotype: Trademark that consists of the company name (Google).

Combination Mark: A combination of these logos (Doritos)

Tip 32: Furniture Legs By the Years

The Caryatid is a furniture leg in the shape of a woman. It was first used in 555 B.C. Up to the 1800s.

Block Foot is a simple square shape used from the 1600s – 1800s.

The Ball foot is a chair leg in the shape of a ball. It was used between 1685-1725 and is one of the earliest chair legs.

Scroll Legs have the design of scrolls at the top and the bottom. This was made during the 1600s.

Spiral Legs are chair legs in the design of a twisted rope, used from 1660-1703.

Trumpet Legs are chair legs with round shapes and flares that actually do resemble a trumpet. They were made from 1600-1750.

A Bun-Foot chair leg resembles a flattened ball and was used from the 1600s-1800s.

Hoof Foot chair legs are just that, the shape of a hoof. They were used between the 1600s – 1700s.

Ball-and-Claw furniture legs are the shape of a claw grasping a ball and used between 1710-1750. This is also called Chippendale furniture.

Bracket Feet has straight corner edges with inner curved edges. This was made in the 1700s.

A Cabriole Leg is a furniture leg that resembles the hind leg of an animal. They were made from 1715-1774.

Fluting is the name for furniture legs that look like parallel columns with concave designs. They were used between the 1700s – 1800s.

Marlborough Legs are straight, square legs used on furniture in the 1700s.

Spider Legs are curved furniture legs at the bottom of round tables. They were made between the 1700s-1800s.

Dolphin Foot chair legs were crafted in the 1700s. They were carved in the shape of a fish head.

Monopodium Foot is the name for chair legs carved to look like the paw of a lion. They were made in the 1800s.

Chapter 3: Know the Value of Your Collectibles

- Collectibles with Mistakes

- Ways to Determine the Value

- Forums, Blogs, and Websites

- Using an Appraiser

- Ways to Spot a Replica

The Value of Your Collectibles

Whether you are buying your collectibles as a financial investment or simply because it is a passion that brings you enjoyment, it is good to know the value of your pieces. There are several ways to learn the value of each piece and a few ways to judge simply by looking at them.

Tip 33: Know the Different Values

Retail Value: This is the price that would be paid in a collectible/antique shop or antique fair.

Wholesale Value: This is the price that the dealer typically pays for the item. This will usually be 33-50 percent less than the retail price.

Fair Market Value – This is the sale price given for an item based on the item's value. This has to be agreed upon by the buyer and the seller.

Insurance Value - This is what the cost would be to replace the item if it was ruined or stolen.

Auction Value – This is the price that would be paid for an item at an auction. This is also known as the open market price.

Tax/Estate Value – This is a value determined by comparing the price paid at an auction for the same item, or something strongly similar.

Tip 34: Mistakes that Increased the Value

When the 50 state quarters were released, it sparked a new set of collectibles. Soon, the images from the state quarters were on beanies and spoons. However, the Kentucky spoon misspelled the state name. On the spoon, it is spelled "KENTUCKEY." Collectors call it the "Spoot" error.

There was another error on a state quarter. This one is on the Kansas quarter. When they were making the Kansas quarters, the "T" on the coin pressing machine had a smudge on it, but they didn't see it before releasing a batch of the quarters. So on some of them instead of having "In God We Trust," it says, "In God We Rust." If you find one, it is worth $100.

Philatelists are always on the lookout for misspellings on stamps. England issued a set on stamps in 2007 that depict England's destination spots. One of those is the "Isle of Wight." However, on the stamp, it reads "Isle of White." The most popular mistake on a stamp is the "Inverted Jenny." This was a 24-cent stamp released in 1918. The blue and red stamp showed the Curtiss JN-4 ("Jenny") airplane flying. But when it was released, the plane was upside-down. They released seven sheets of the stamp, with each sheet containing 100 stamps. The government was able to destroy six sheets. The seventh was sold to a stamp collector, William Robey. He separated the stamps and sold them individually.

In 1865, the Griswold Company released the "Square baking Skillet." But the first few that were released are missing the "E" on the end, and the pan shows "Squar Baking Skillet. The one with the error is worth twice as much.

The 1910 baseball card for Sherwood "Sherry" Magee is misspelled, and his last name shows as "Magie." This mistake made it one of the most valuable baseball cards by Topps, even in poor condition.

Tip 35: Recognizable Ty Beanie Errors

Beanie Babies were thought to be the next sought after collectible, but the value has since gone down on them. However, a few still carry a high sticker value, especially the ones with an error. There were 2,000 baby elephant beanies made that were royal blue in color and named "Peanuts." There was a manufacturing error that caused the beanie to be a darker color than they wanted. That beanie is now worth nearly $5,000.

There are beanies with name errors on the tags. The first spelling error was to a lobster named "Pinchers." On some of the tags, it reads "Punchers." Other mistakes include a duck named "Quackers" whos is missing the "s" so it reads as "Quacker." There is a ghost named "Spooky." The earlier beanies are spelled, "Spook." There is "Tusk," the walrus that was misspelled to read, "Tuck."

Tip 36: Restorations Could Devalue Your Collectible

Condition matters! If the item has extensive damage, you may have to restore the piece. In some cases, this could cause the product to devalue, especially if you remove important markings. Before you attempt any restorations, have the item appraised to see if restoring the piece will lower the value. If the damage is extensive, restorations may be necessary.

The purpose of restorations is to preserve the original look. If you notice the piece has been painted several times, it is fair to say the original look has probably been covered up by now. This mostly happens with items that are wooden or enamel. In that case, it has lost much of the value. Consult a professional before you begin restoration projects. They can inform you of what you need to do. If you plan to restore antique silver pieces, paintings, and prints, it is always better to go with a professional.

Tip 37: How Bakelite Became a Valued Collectible

Bakelite was the first type of plastic that would not melt at high temperatures. It was created by Dr. Leo Baekeland in 1907. It was popular from the 1930s – 1950s and was called "art plastic." Today it is often referred to as "phenolic resin." They cut back on making Bakelite during World War II due to a shortage of necessary ingredients. By the end of the war, they stopped making it altogether. Some products made from Bakelite are jewelry, flatware handles, salt & pepper shakers, buttons, lighters, dominoes, perfume bottles, and even pencil sharpeners. It was one of the earliest forms of Bakelite and often called "art plastic." Through the years, collectors have found a new desire for Bakelite, and the value has skyrocketed. For example, a brooch that first sold for 79 cents, will sell today for $400.

Tip 38: What is Your Collectible Made of?

It is essential to know what your collectible is made of; it greatly impacts the value. Whether those collectibles include figurines, egg cups, or even toothpick holders, take note of what was used to craft the item. Each and everything you collect was made from some type of material, and it is important to know a little about that. For example, pewter looks like silver but as a lighter feel to it. Pewter is made up of tin, antinomy, and copper. Because of this, it will never rust or tarnish over the years.

Some people collect specific material products, such as pewter items, crystal, Bakelite, or even a favorite type of wood. Others collect objects such as paperweights, vases, or ring holders. It could be that someone who collects ring holders may want to add one made of pewter. Or someone who collects paperweights may wish to add a crystal paperweight for their collection.

Those collectors may want to add a pewter ring holder or a crystal paperweight. When you know the history of the material that is used, you can classify your treasured pieces and get an accurate value.

Some of the more popular styles of glassware and figurines are silver, pewter, ivory, and wrought iron. There are collectibles made with a pattern that gave the item its name.

Brass was made in 1781 when zinc was added to liquid copper.

Transferware is what collectors refer to as ceramics decorated with motifs.

Favrile Glass is an iridescent glass created by Louis Comfort Tiffany to be used in his lamps.

Crackle Glass is a glass product with the look of tiny cracks covering it. It was first produced in 1877.

An aluminum product hammered into shape is known as "hammered aluminum."

Goofus Glass is pressed glass with painted designs. It was made from 1897-1920's.

Chalkware is a form of Plaster-of-Paris that is painted with oils and watercolors.

Fiestaware is ceramic glazed dinnerware by the Homer Laughlin China Company.

Belleek is an eggshell-thin porcelain with an iridescent clear glaze.

Rockingham Ware – Pottery covered with streaks of brown glaze.

Carnival Glass is pressed glass made in the early 1900s until 1930. They were re-introduced by the Imperial Glass Company in the 1950s. The idea of carnival glass was so that families could afford beautiful glassware. The items were purchased at carnivals across the United States, earning the name Carnival Glass.

Depression Glass was glassware made during the Depression, from the late 1920s to the late 1940s. It is described as colorful yet clear glassware. Their first colors were pink, green, cobalt blue, amber, and yellow. Crystal was produced in the 1930s. It got its start as a promotional item given away with a purchase or service.

Tip 39: Know Your Colored Collectibles

There are collectors who seek specific "Colored Collectibles." Knowing the history behind the colored pieces will also tell you much about the value.

Milk Glass dates back to Egypt in 1500 BC. An Italian book published in 1612 gave the recipe for milk glass. It was first made in America in 1939 by the Fenton Glass Company. It was initially called Milk Glass because of the deep white look. Before 1960 it was iridized, giving it a rainbow effect on the surface. Colors range from thick white, grayish or bluish opalescent, green, pink, blue, and lavender.

Custard Glass was introduced in England in the 1890s. Vaseline Glass was made from 1880 and up until World War II. It was re-introduced in 1959. They were given those names based on the color of the glass.

Cranberry Glass also earned its name from the color. It can range from pink to burgundy. Other types of collectibles that are named after their color are Jade (green), Cobalt (blue), and Opalescent (light blue).

Alabaster is typically white or tan in color. It is a soft material and can be carved in any form, from vases and lamps to figurines.

Tip 40: Forums for Collectors

There are several forums that can be used to find the value of your piece. On Antiquers.com, Treasure Net, Worth Point, and Old Shop Stuff collectors can upload a photo of their item to gain information on the item's history and value from fellow collectors.

The Houzz.com forum helps in several ways. Members can walk you through the steps of restoring collectibles. They can also help you to age and find the value of your piece.

The iantiqueonline.ning.com forum offers an abundance of information. Along with helping to collect information on your collectible, there are links to buy and sell your pieces, and classes on various subjects of antiques and collectibles. There is also a chance to join groups of collectors with similar interests.

Tip 41: Collectors Blogs To Follow

At Blog.chasenantiques.com and loveantiques.com collectors can find an abundance of information on their pieces. Both sites touch on a wide variety of collectibles that include in-depth details on their history and value. For collectors of antique and vintage jewelry, I recommend the blogs agelessheirlooms.com and lillicoco.com/blogs/love-lillicoco-blog.

Tip 42: Internet Sites to Value Collectibles

If beanies are what you collect, the website, Love My Beanies (www.lovemybeanies.com), provides an excellent price guide that will give the value of your bean-filled pieces.

There may be times when you want to determine the value of your antique or collectible but cannot make it out to an appraiser. In that case, you can have it done online at the website, "Value My Stuff." This is convenient and can be done online by merely uploading your photos. The appraisal only takes 24-48 hours.

Some collectibles have an established price guideline that can be found online. The Kovels' Antiques and Collectibles Price Guide shows the sales prices of over 700 categories of antiques and collectibles. This can be found on their website: Kovels.com. The website Beckett.com can give the most accurate information on trading cards, baseball cards, sports memorabilia, and coins.

Tip 43: Why an Appraiser?

You can get a fair estimated value of an item from an appraiser. They are more impartial than a person from an antique store or a dealer because they are ethically bound from purchasing an item after they make an appraisal. Bank managers and estate attorneys can also refer you to a reputable appraiser. When you work with an online appraiser, choose one that is certified by the American Society of Appraisers, the Appraisers Association of America, or the International Society of Appraisers. The costs of working with an appraiser will vary between $150-$350 an hour, depending on experience and accreditation. Do not work with an Appraiser of charges a percentage of the item's value.

Some auction houses have Appraisal Day, and you can meet reputable appraisers. They also have Valuation days where you can get an appraisal for free.

Tip 44: What an Appraiser Looks For

There are ten factors that will determine the value of your item.

Is it an original piece or a reproduction?

What is the history of the item? Who owned it previously?

How many were produced and how many survived?

Does it still work properly? Does any part of it still work?

Is there a demand for the item? Would collectors or museums be interested?

Is it attractive? Will it fit well as a display? Does it make a good conversation piece?

What is the condition? Are there chips, scratches, cracks, or discoloration? Has it been restored?

Is the item complete with all of its original parts? Does it have the box and instructions? If it is part of a set, do you have all of the pieces?

Is it signed? Is the company/maker well known? Does it have markings, labels, or identifying numbers?

The core question is, what is the item worth to you? Does it have any sentimental value?

Tip 45: Other Factors that Determine the Value

Other than the standardized rules for determining an item's value, there are more attributes that can influence the value of a collectible. The first is whether one or both sides may prefer to go with the amount listed in a Price Guide or a separate agreed upon amount. The second is that the buyer may have a price in mind that they want to pay. There may be an amount that they cannot go over based on their own finances. The third is what obstacles the buyer or seller is going through to obtain the item, such as, shipping expenses, postage, travel costs, or legal paperwork.

Tip 46: YouTube Shows Just for Collectors

YouTube is a hot spot of information on any subject, from religion and recipes to pet care and even how to find a lost cell phone. As for collectors, there are several channels that will be helpful to collectors.

Antiquesarena: This show has a treasure trove of videos on buying and restoring antiques and collectibles.

DenverBrassArmadillo: They list dozens of amazing videos on a wide variety of collectibles.

Curiosity Incorporated: Chris is an antique enthusiast who posts videos that explore junkyards, forgotten places, and discuss collectible history.

Dr. Lori: She is the star appraiser on Auction Kings. Her videos provide a wealth of information on collecting, buying, selling, spotting a fake, and much more!

These YouTube shows are steeped in knowledge about antiques, so when you watch their videos, you may want to take notes. The videos on these three shows just might motivate you to start a whole new collection.

Tip 47: Replica vs. Original

Many companies started making replicas. This was done for several reasons. People admired collectibles that they could not find or afford. Some made the replicas to fool collectors into paying higher prices for newer items, believing that they were antiques. Here are a few ways to tell the replicas apart from the originals.

In artwork, there are several ways to tell if it is a replica. There will be more than one signature. It will be behind glass, and there is a reproduction number, such as 38/100. That tells you that was the 38th painting produced in a series of 100. Another way is if you look under a magnifying glass, you will see colored dots. There are also signs that will tell you if the painting is an original. It is on canvas. There is only one signature. You can see texture and brush strokes, particularly under a magnifying glass.

Crazing is a name for the hairline cracks that appear after firing. Sometimes it shows years later. Crazing can lower the value, but it can be fixed. Some people add crazing to make an item look older. Purposely added crazing is equal in line width and color. Crazing that appears naturally is more random.

On imitation pieces of items, such as clocks and small furniture, there are cut lines embedded in the wood that shows where the wood was supposed to be cut by the maker. Original pieces will never have cut lines.

Small shallow jars have lids that have become collectibles on their own. Many of these lids have chips. Inside the chip, there should be yellowing from age. If there is no discoloration from aging, then it is most likely a replica.

Tip 48: Toy Prizes that are now Collectibles

Toys started becoming hot collectibles in the 1970s. Each decade brings on a whole new line of toys that grow in value. A specific type of toy that has become a category of its own are the prizes! There are toys given to children with their restaurant meals, the ones buried in cereal boxes, and the most popular of all – the toys in the Cracker Jack boxes.

Burger Chef was the first restaurant to offer kids meals that came with a toy. It was called the "Fun Meal." It came with a burger, french fries, dessert, and toy. They were open from 1954-1973. After the burger chain closed, McDonald's followed with their Happy Meal in 1979. The toys included in the first Happy Meal were a McDoodle Stencil, ID Bracelet, Puzzle Lock, Spinning Top, Ronald McDonald Eraser, and a McWrist Wallet.

It was Kellogg's that started the trend of putting prizes in cereal boxes in 1909. The first prize was the book, The Funny Jungleland Moving Pictures Book, and was given to customers at the store who purchased two boxes of Kellogg's cereal. That changed shortly after and customers would have to mail UPC codes and a dime to get their book. In the 1930s, General Mills was the first to put prizes inside the box. It was a set of eight Skippy cards that came inside their box of Wheaties.

German immigrant Frederick Ruechkeim, his brother Louis, and his partner William Brinkmeyer introduced Cracker Jacks in 1873. At that time, the words "cracker jack" was an expression that described something wonderful. Cracker Jack started adding toys to their boxes in 1912. The first prizes were a set of baseball cards. The Cracker Jack mascot, Sailor Jack, was introduced in 1916. He was designed in the image of Rueckheim's 8-year-old grandson, Robert, who passed away from pneumonia.

Chapter 4: Know These Collectible Firsts

- Recognizing Pottery and Porcelain

- Promotional Characters and Mascots

- History of Premiums and Toys

- Timeline to the Automobile

- Firsts in Toys and Fashion

The Importance of History

Behind each and every collectible is a story about how the item got its start if you are lucky enough to find that FIRST one than your collection will shine for sure! These are collectible firsts under different categories that you just may find on your search for new collectibles. Keep in mind that these items stand out for their popularity in the collectibles community and because they can fall under several categories. This information will help you in your search. Once again, it is also important to know descriptive details, so you know that the piece you are buying is authentic.

Tip 49: The Beginning of Pottery

There are three types of ceramic material:

Earthenware: This is coarse-grained

Stoneware: Used to make pottery.

Porcelain (Kaolin): Delicate and fine-grained

Earthenware is also known as terra cotta, and kaolin is also known as china clay. Stoneware pottery was made from the 1900-1940s. This included the popular "spongeware" collection. These pieces look like they were actually dabbed with a sponge. Pottery is created when the clay is baked to form a glass-like material. The Hittite Civilization first used it from 1400-1200 BC Stoneware is best known for making jars, jugs, jardinieres, and steins. The difference between a jug and a jardiniere is that a jug has a spout and one handle, and a jardiniere has a handle on each side and a circular opening on top (no spout).

Pottery items were once nicknamed, "Bluebirds" because production ran between fall and spring, the time when bluebirds returned from the south. Majolica is a tin-glazed pottery introduced by the Islamic in the 10th century. One of the well-known pottery makers was the Hull Pottery Company from Roseville, Ohio. It opened in the 1880s and closed in the 1970s. When they first opened, they made Stoneware. Mottoware is pottery decorated with words or initials.

Tip 50: The Story Behind Porcelain

Bisque is unglazed porcelain. Porcelain was first made in China between 1280 and 1367. It made its appearance with the origin of the Ming Dynasty. It was first made in the United States between 1710 and 1718. Bone China was first made in 1800. Bone China is made from a soft porcelain that includes a paste that is mixed with bone-ash. Adding the bone-ash produced a strong white porcelain. The oldest porcelain manufacturer in America is Cybis Porcelain.

Mottoware is porcelain with words or initials written on them. Flow Blue porcelain was created by accident. While making the blue pottery, the ink ran in certain spots that darkened the blue and gave it a smeared look. The pieces look like they were left out in the rain, and the color ran. Customers loved the appearance, and it quickly earned the name Flow Blue.

Tip 51: What You Should Know about the Glaze

Glaze is a glossy film that is applied to a ceramic during firing. There are several ways this can be done: with a brush, a spray, being poured on, or the item can be dipped into the glaze.

Slip is a type of glaze used for Earthenware. The pottery is then referred to as Slipware. The clear glaze is what gives it a yellow color. Earthenware would not be able to hold liquids without the glaze. There are four types of glaze: lead glaze, tin glaze, salt glaze, and crackle glaze. When a decoration is added on top of the glaze before it is fired, the border stands out, visually, and can sometimes be felt. This is called an "overglazed decoration."

Tip 52: Retired Sports Memorabilia

Before the start of the Olympic games, we are introduced to a new mascot – a new collectible! The first Olympic mascot was Schuss, a depiction of a man on skis and painted in blue, red, and white, the colors of France. He debuted in January 1967 as a representative of the 1968 Grenoble Olympic Games. Schuss was the start of an Olympic trend.

All of Hawaii's college teams were once referred to as Fighting Rainbows, depicted by a rainbow. In 2000, many started to complain about their team being represented by a symbol that was later adopted by the gay community. Some of the team names are now called "Warriors" or "Rainbows" they are currently represented by "Vili the Warrior." Their new colors are black, green, and white.

On February 1, 1963, the Florida Technological Institute opened its doors in Melbourne. Their mascot was a Citronaut – a character with an orange for a body and an alien head. This gave a nod to Florida's orange crops and the country's ever-growing space program. In 1968, the school changed its name to the University of Central Florida. While revamping the school, the students voted on a new mascot. Their choices were a "Knight of Pegasus" or Vincent the Vulture." The Pegasus won as the new school mascot.

During the 1966 baseball season, the Pittsburgh Pirates had their own lucky charm, known as the Green Weenie. The gimmick was a creation of Bob Prince (Pirates broadcaster) and Danny Whelan (Pirates Trainer). It was only used for three months but has earned a page in the book of iconic mascots.

The University of Mississippi (Ole Miss) adopted a mascot in 1973, a Confederate soldier named Colonel Reb. Despite being loved by students and fans, the school decided to replace him in 2003 due to pressure by groups claiming it was insensitive to have a Confederate soldier as a mascot. Fans continued to support Colonel Red until 2011 when they banned the sale of all Colonel Red merchandise. He was replaced with the Rebel Black Bear in 2010.

Tip 53: Collectible Advertising Characters and Mascots

A variety of advertising icons have spun into today's collectibles. They are also "cross collectibles" because they are sought after by people looking for other than Mascots. For example, let us say that someone collects dolls, and then adds a Campbell's Kids doll to their collection. That doll has a higher value than other dolls because it also depicts Campbell's mascot.

Bibendum, also known as the Michelin Man, was the idea of Édouard Michelin, company founder. He saw a stack of tires that he thought looked like a person – thus, the Michelin Man was born in 1898. He has gone through numerous incarnations. After the 1920s, he was no longer seen drinking alcohol or smoking and appeared in ads playing sports. Creator Eileen Gray crafted the Bibendum chair in the early 1900s. In 1986, Sir Terence Conran and Lord Paul Hamlyn opened the Bibendum Restaurant and Oyster Bar in London.

Smokey Bear: He was created by the U.S. Forest Service and the Ad Council to create a campaign to educate the public on how they can prevent forest fires. He first appeared on August 9, 1944.

Procter & Gamble: The Mr. Clean man was the brainchild of Harry Barnhart in 1957. Ernie Allen from the art department of Tatham-Laird & Kudner in 1957. Chicago, Illinois, gave life to Barnhart's idea.

Morris the Cat: Morris made his debut in 1968. He was a mascot for 9 Lives for ten years. Morris was rescued from the Humane Society of Hinsdale, Illinois, by his handler Bob Martwick. He was searching for an orange cat for the 9 Lives commercials.

Drumming Bunny: In 1973, Mallory Duracell created the Drumming Bunny for their commercial. In 1988, their trademark lapsed. Energizer stepped in and created a similar mascot of a pink bunny wearing black sunglasses.

Tip 54: Timeline of Cereal Mascots

When it comes to mascots, the cereal mascots seem to always rise in value, especially if you can include those extra special premiums that were often buried inside the cereal. Today, there are more retired cereal mascots than there are current ones. It is essential to note the years that their images changed. This is important when judging the item's age. These are some of the treasured cereal mascots in the collector's world.

Rice Krispies: They first sold in 1928. Snap was introduced as their first mascot in 1932. He was a gnome in a baker's hat. In 1938, Crackle and Pop were added. In 1949, The Snap, Crackle, and Pop characters were given a makeover to look more human.

Frosted Flakes: When Kellogg's Sugar Frosted Flakes of Corn debuted in 1952, they had several mascots, that included, Tony the Tiger, Newt the Gnu, Elmo the Elephant, and Katy the Kangaroo. They had a competition where shoppers could vote for their favorite character. Tony the Tiger won and is still the mascot to this day. A trademark of Tony's iconic image is his blue nose!

Sugar Smacks: In 1953, Sugar Smacks debuted with their first mascot, Cliffy the Clown. The character was discontinued in 1956. He was replaced with Sammy the Seal from 1957-1961. Quick Draw McGraw was next in their line of mascots from 1961-1965. The Smackin' Brothers were introduced in 1966. In 1971, the cereal was represented by a Native American Chief. This only lasted a year. It was in 1972 that Dig'em Frog was introduced.

Cocoa Puffs cereal was introduced in 1956. Their mascot, Sonny the Cuckoo Bird, made his debut in 1962, wearing a pink and white striped shirt and a bow tie. From 1970-1995, he wore a striped turtle neck shirt. From 1995-2004, he was giving a softer appearance, with bigger eyes and a larger beak. He wore a shirt and jacket, but the striped shirt was gone. After 2004, his beak was made smaller, and they removed the shirt altogether.

Tricks, the Trix Rabbit, debuted in 1959. When the cereal was introduced in 1954, they had three colors: red (raspberry), orange, and yellow. Through the years, other colors and flavors were added that include grape, wildberry blue, lime, watermelon, and berry blue. In 2017, when Trix announced they would no longer use artificial flavors, they went back to four colors: orange, yellow, red, and purple.

Sugar Pops cereal sponsored the Adventures of Wild Bill Hickok radio and television show that ran from April 15, 1951-September 24, 1958. During those years, Guy Madison, the star of the show, appeared on the corn pops box. The slogan on the box was, "Shoot it with Sugar." In 1959, after the show went off the air, Sugar Pops Pete took over as the cereal mascot until 1967; still using the slogan, "shoot it with sugar." Big Yella was the Corn Pops mascot from 1977-1980. To make sure your collectible is not a replica, you will want to note their name changes. The cereal changed names almost as often as they changed mascots.

Kellogg's introduced Corn Pops in 1950 and changed the name to Sugar Corn Pops a year later, in 1951. The name was changed once more, in 1978, to Sugar Pops. In 1984, it was changed back to Corn Pops, when cereal companies were dropping the word "Sugar" from their names. In January 2006, it was changed Briefly to "Pops." Buyers did not like it, and the name was quickly switched back to Corn Pops.

In 1963, Lucky Charms was introduced with their mascot, Lucky the Leprechaun. Through the years, he went by the names LC Leprechaun and Sir Charms. It was the first cereal to include marshmallows. In 1975, Lucky was replaced with Waldo the Wizard. That lasted several months before Lucky returned.

Fruit Loops cereal was first sold in 1963. Their mascot Toucan Sam, a blue Toucan bird, has always been the only mascot for Fruit Loops.

Captain Crunch cereal was introduced in 1963. Their mascot, a Captain, named "Horatio Magellan Crunch," had his backstory. To teach children his story, he appeared in a series of commercials with Rocky and Bullwinkle. It was then that children learned he was Captain of the ship, the Guppy. He was born on Crunch Island, a magical island in the Sea of Milk, off the coast of Ohio that was home to the mountain, Mt Crunchmore.

Sugar Crisp cereal adopted Sugar Bear as their mascot in 1965. Sugar Bear was a part of the first animated commercial to air on TV. The main reason was to add characters to Post's new cartoon, Linus the Lionhearted. It was a TV show full of cereal mascots. The cartoon went off the air in 1966, but Sugar Bear remains the mascot for the cereal whose name changed to Golden Crisp in 1985.

Quisp vs. Quake vs. Quangaroo: In 1965, Quaker introduced Quisp and Quake cereals. They were promoted together and competed against each other in commercials. In 1969, Quake had a makeover to his appearance. He was now slimmer and wore an Australian bush hat instead of a miner's helmet. In 1972, they held a contest to see which one the children liked more. Quake lost, and the cereal was discontinued. The day the commercial aired announcing that he lost, Quake introduced his new sidekick. Simon the kangaroo, and his new cereal, Quangaroos. The first box of Quangaroos cereal shows both Quake and Simon, side-by-side. In 1979, they had another vote to see which cereal the children liked more: Quisp or Quangaroos. Simon lost, and Quangaroos cereal was discontinued.

Frankenberry and Count Chocula were introduced in March 1971. Boo Berry joined the team in December 1973. Fruit Brute, a werewolf, was launched in 1974 but discontinued in 1982. The Fruity Yummy Mummy debuted in 1987 but was discontinued only five years later in 1992.

Sir Grapefellow cereal was only sold in 1972. The mascot was a British World War I pilot. The cereal may have been short-lived, but there were still several pieces of memorabilia made that are sought after by collectors.

The original Cookie Crisp mascot was Cookie Jarvis (1977 - 1983). He was a wizard with a wand, long robe, pointy hat, and big white beard. Both the wand and the pointy hat were decorated with chocolate-covered chocolate chip cookies. Beginning in 1981, they added Cookie Crook and Cookie Cop (Officer Crumb). In 1990, they gave Cookie Crook a sidekick named Chip, the dog.

Honey Nut Cheerios was first sold in 1979. Though the box featured the mascot, Buzz, he did not have a name until 2000. They held a nationwide contest to name the bee. Kristine Tong, a fifth-grader in Coolidge, Texas, won. Her name for the cereal mascot was – BuzzBee! Several months later, they shortened his name to Buzz.

The cereal also went through name changes. In 1982, the cereal name was changed to Honey Smacks, and then to Smacks in the 1990s. In 2004, it was changed back to Honey Smacks. In Germany, Spain, Belgium, the Netherlands, and France, it is still sold with the name "Smacks."

Big Mixx – This cereal was released in 1990 and discontinued in 1992. The Big Mixx character was a combination of a chicken, moose, pig, and wolf.

Tip 55: History of Food and Beverage Mascots

This is a timeline of food and beverage mascots. These characters have been emblazoned on cookie jars, spoons, toys, salt and pepper shakers, recipe boxes, ornaments, stickers, bells, dolls, banks, and much more.

Campbell's Soup: In 1904, the Campbell's Kids sprang from the pen of Grace Drayton, an Illustrator for the Philadelphia Press and Evening Journal and also a children's book illustrator. There are 16 different Campbell's Kids. They first appeared on streetcars and in magazine advertisements.

Morton Salt: The Morton Salt Umbrella Girl appeared in 1914. There have been seven versions of the Salt Girl. The first was a girl in a yellow dress and yellow knee socks, holding a yellow umbrella. Her image was redesigned in 1921, 1933, 1941, 1956, 1968, and once more in 2014 to celebrate her 100 years.

Planters: In 1916, Planters held a competition for a new advertising icon. It was won by thirteen-year-old, Antonio Gentile, with his creation of Mr. Peanut. His prize for the contest was $5. However, most people do not know that Amedeo Obici, founder of Planters, also paid for Gentile's, and his four siblings to go to college.

The Jolly Green Giant mascot was introduced in 1928. His features went through several changes. When he was first introduced, he was a white man with black hair, holding a large pod of peas. In 1930, he was colored in completely green. In 1936, he was made taller and was now holding a giant corn cob. In 1960, he was drawn a little taller, was standing upright and facing forward, was no longer holding a vegetable, and his arms were crossed at his chest. He was also now wearing a scarf. In 1976, his image was changed again. The Jolly Green Giant was now standing with his hands on his hips, and he was facing the right. He was no longer wearing a red scarf and was now wearing pointed, ankle-high, green shoes. Today there is a 55-foot statue of the Jolly Green Giant in Blue Earth, Minnesota. Every winter, they place a giant red scarf around his neck.

Oscar Mayer Weinermobile: This first Weinermobile was created in 1936. It was designed by Oscar Mayer's nephew, Carl G Mayer, and was smaller than the one that we see today. The Weinermobile was redesigned in 1958. That is the one that is still used today.

Cheetos: Charles Elmer Doolin invented Cheetos in 1948. Their first advertising icon was Cheetos Mouse. He was used from 1971-1979. Chester Cheetah was introduced in 1986.

Starkist: Charlie the Tuna was introduced as the Starkist mascot in 1961. When the company refused to start a fan club for collectors of Charlie the Tuna memorabilia, a fan started the Sorry Charlie No-fan-club-for-you Club. April 6th is now marked as National Sorry Charlie Day.

Hostess: Twinkie the Kid: In1971, when Twinkie the Kid debuted, he was wearing a blue bandanna with red spots. He was pulled from 1988-1990. When

Twinkie the Kid was brought back, his bandanna now said, "Hostess."

Hawaiian Punch: Punchy, the "Hawaiian Punch guy," was the brainchild of the Atherton-Privett advertising agency in December 1961. Artist, Martin Mandelblatt gave life to Punchy in February 1962.

Pillsbury: The Pillsbury Doughboy made his debut on November 7, 1965. Commercials for the Doughboy were stepping stones for the careers of actors Michael Cera, Kirsten Dunst, Maureen McCormick, and Drew Barrymore.

Keebler Elves: The first was J.J. Keebler. He was introduced in 1969. Thirteen more elves were added on through the years, each with their own role.

Nesquik Rabbit: The Nestle Quik bunny named, Quiky, was introduced in 1973. He was brandished with a Q on his chest. In 1999, the Q was changed to an N.

Bud Light: Spuds MacKenzie, a bull terrier, first appeared on their commercial during the Super Bowl in 1987 and was an overnight sensation. Republican Senator Strom Thurmond accused Anheuser-Busch of using the dog to encourage underage drinking. Mothers Against Drunk Driving launched a campaign asking schools to ban spuds MacKenzie apparel. The Spuds MacKenzie dog was discontinued in 1989.

Tip 56: A Lesson in Restaurant Mascots

Famous restaurant mascots include:

Big Boy (Bog Boy's Restaurant) 1936

Spee-dee (McDonald's) 1948

Jack (Jack-in-the-Box) 1951

The King (Burger King) 1955

Ronald McDonald (McDonald's) 1963

Wendy (Wendy's Restaurant) 1969

The Bee (Jollibee) 1980

Clara Peller - Where's the Beef? (Wendy's) 1984

There are several types of restaurant collectors. Those who collect menus, glasses, caps, restaurant ware, and memorabilia in general either from several restaurants or one in particular or a favorite mascot. Here is a timeline and facts of several restaurants, some of which are closed. This information can help to age your collectibles and further your research. In 1952, when Kentucky Fried Chicken first opened, the face of Colonel Sanders became the first restaurant mascot. The Pig Stand opened in 1921 and was the first "drive-in" restaurant. This was the practice of waitresses bringing food to your car. In 1951, Jack-in-the-Box Restaurants started the concept of the "drive-thru." These are several restaurant mascots.

During the 1980s, Domino's Pizza created the Noid to represent the pizza chain. The Noid is a character wearing a rabbit-eared bodysuit. The Noid was discontinued in 1995. He has since made brief appearances for celebratory reasons. Among Noid collectors, items are several video games.

There is a restaurant mistake that stirred a phenomenal children's restaurant and whole new collectible. In 1977, restaurant owners wanted to purchase a coyote costume for their new restaurant – Coyote Pizza. They mistakenly ordered a mouse. The character Chuck E. Cheese did not become the official mascot until 1980. Before that, he was just one of the restaurant's characters. The concept of mixing the restaurant with an arcade was the idea of Atari Co-founder, Nolan Bushnell.

Tip 57: Timeline to the Automobile

Knowing the timeline of changes made to different automobiles will help with several collectibles. The collectibles community is a mixture of fun and knowledgeable peer groups who enjoy sharing their passions. However, among the group are sharks that will try to con you into purchasing items at a higher price, claiming they are older than they actually are.

Transportation collectors search for automobile memorabilia, transportation novelty items, specific models, hood ornaments, license plates, car/truck parts, and the actual automobiles themselves. And it all started in 3000 BC with the invention of the horse-drawn carriage. It was also known as the "chariot" and later called the "horse-and-buggy." In 1838, Lord Broughman created the carriage as we know it to look today. In the 19th century, Obadiah Elliot improved the carriage by adding steel springs. Changes made to the carriage throughout the 18th century included the creation of the Phaeton, one of the first automobiles. The Studebaker Company is the only carriage manufacturer to switch from making horse-drawn carriages to cars successfully.

Speedometers – 1901

Rear View Mirror – 1911

Car Heaters – 1917

Four-Wheel Brakes - 1923

Back-Up Lights – 1923

Semi-Automatic Car – 1926

Convertible Top – 1927

Power steering – 1951

Cruise Control - 1957

Front Seat Shoulder Seat Belts – 1967

In 1901, New York made a law that automobile owners had to put their initials on their cars. They used metal letters on leather pads, which cost $1. This was the introduction of the license plate. Those original license plates are highly sought after by collectors. The driver's license was introduced in 1906 and cost $1. Stop Signs were first used in 1914, and the traffic light was introduced in 1919.

In 1910, BF Goodrich tried an experiment with their tires to see if the public would like tires that were a different color. They added carbon pigments (used by Binney & Smith to make Crayola crayons) to make the white tires - black. He found that the pigments gave the tires abrasion resistance, making them stronger and more durable.

William Harley and Arthur Davidson sold their first Harley-Davidson motorcycle in 1903. The first Harley-Davidson Motor Company was in a wooden shed in Milwaukee, Wisconsin.

In 1920, they started holding races and used a pig as their mascot. After each win, they would carry the pig during their victory lap, earning the name, "the Hog." They began making their gas tanks in a teardrop shape in 1925. They added the eagle to their tanks in 1933.

Cars were first wired for radio in 1929, though the radio was sold separately. In 1937 the gear shift was moved from the floor to the steering column. Sealed headlights and tubeless tires were added in the 1940s. In 1948 Cadillac created the first automobile with "tailfins." In 1949 Chrysler made the first automobile that started by turning a key only. In 1955 they made an automobile equipped with a record player. GM was the first to install airbags in 1973.

Tip 58: Transportation Firsts

These "first moments" in the automobile industry are essential to take note of in your research. These are the years that different types of vehicles were introduced to the world.

First motorcycle – 1885

Tractor Trailers - 1896

Delivery Trucks - 1896

First bus – 1900

Pickup truck - 1917

Mini Van - 1935

Charles and Frank Duryea opened the Duryea Motor Wagon Company in 1893. He started selling his automobiles in 1900 in Reading, Pennsylvania. They were the first to sell a car in America. They were open for three years and sold 13 vehicles. Their first automobile is in the Smithsonian.

Tip 59: How Premiums Became Collectibles

Premiums are the samples/merchandise that businesses pass out, usually with the company name on it. Not all of them have the company name. Some are gifts that are given to reward customers. If you look into the history of your collectibles, you will find which companies offered premiums along the way. These premiums have become collectibles themselves. Some of those premiums spun off into an entire business.

William Wrigley Sr. established the Wrigley Manufacturing Company that sold several products for the home, such as toothpaste and soap (their best-seller). Selling soap was the first job he gave to his 13-years-old son, William Wrigley Jr. when he went to work for him. He could be spotted every day, walking up and down the Philadelphia streets, selling his soap from a basket. He continued to sell the soap, and, as a premium, he offered a bag of baking powder to customers as an incentive. When customers became bigger fans of the baking powder than the soap, he decided to switch and sell the baking powder with an offer of gum as a gift to customers. Once again, the customers preferred the premium over the products he was selling. He decided to go into the chewing gum business full time. In 1893, he sold his first two chewing gum brands: Juicy Fruit and Wrigley's Spearmint.

David H. McConnel was a door-to-door book salesman in 1886. To increase sales, he offered a small bottle of perfume as a premium. Customers loved the fragrance so much that they would buy a book just to get the perfume. Realizing this, McConnel shifted from selling books to bottles of perfume. He created the perfumes, mixing the fragrances, himself. In September of 1886, McConnel launched the California Perfume Company at 126 Chambers Street in

Manhattan, New York. He changed the name of the company to "Avon" in 1892. He hired Mrs. PFE Albee as his first Sales Representative. They released their first brochure in 1896. And to think, it all started with a perfume premium. In 1997, Mattel teamed with Avon to produce a line of Mrs. PFE Albee Barbie Dolls. Each year, Avon gifts their top sellers with a Mrs. PFE Albee porcelain doll. And it all started with a perfume premium.

Tip 60: Fashion Firsts All Collectors Should Know

The first hoop skirt was made in 1470. It was worn by Queen Juana so that she could hide her pregnancy.

The first high heeled shoes were made in the 15th Century for Persian soldiers. It was so their feet would fit more securely in the horse stirrups. In the 1600s, a woman was photographed wearing heels at a wedding. She wanted to look taller. Soon, other women were wearing them for fashion purposes, so the men stopped wearing them.

Jeans were first made in 1874 by Levi Strauss and Jacob Davis. Whitcomb Judson developed the zipper in 1893. It was first called the "clasp locker."

The US Rubber Company made the first sneakers in America in 1943. The shoes were called Keds.

T-shirts were first made in 1898. They were given their name based on their "T" shape. In 1913, the US

Navy started wearing them under their uniforms. In 1938, Sears advertised T-shirts as clothing that could be worn on its own.

Maybelline was the first line of makeup. It was created by Chicago chemist Thomas Williams for his older sister, Maybel, in 1913. She was using petroleum jelly to enhance her eyelashes and eyebrows but was looking for something different. They first sold their makeup by mail order.

Tip 61: Mistakes that Became Collectible Toys

The toy collectors have had their share of accidental collectibles. Play-Doh was initially a wallpaper cleaner that was rolled on the walls to remove coal dust.

The first commercial for a toy was for Mr. Potato Head. When it was introduced in 1952, it was just the facial pieces that were sold. Children would stick them in actual potatoes. They did not include the plastic potato until 1964.

The Ancient Greeks made the first Yo-Yos with terracotta in 500 BC When Pedro Flores immigrated to America from the Philippines in 1915, he brought the toy with him. However, at the time, it was called a "bandalore." Flores gave it the name Yo-Yo which means "come-come" in his language. He worked at a bellhop at a hotel in California and would show off his tricks with the toy to the guests. One of those guests was Donald Duncan, who then bought him out in 1920.

The Slinky is another one of them! In 1943, naval engineer Richard James was working when a spring fell off his workbench and began to "walk" across the floor. As he watched it slink away, he thought about making a toy out of it. His wife, Betty, thought of the name Slinky. The toy was released in 1945. In 1960, despite his success, Richard James was suffering from a serious mid-life crisis. He left the company, his wife, and six children for a Bolivian religious cult. His wife, Betty James, took over as the head of James Industries. She was responsible for the additions to the Slinky line, including Slinky Jr., Plastic Slinky, Slinky Dog, Slinky Pets, Crazy Slinky Eyes, and Neon Slinky. In 2001, Betty was inducted into the Toy Industry Hall of Fame.

Silly Putty was intended for use by the military. During World War II, the military put out a request for a new type of rubber. Scientists across the country got to work at it, including Dr. James Wright. After he mixed boric acid to silicone oil, he found it made a unique texture of rubber. Though it was resilient, it had a risk of melting and would not hold a shape. Since it could not be used, he put it aside on top of a few newspapers. When he peeled it off later, he saw that the images from the paper stuck to it. And the world now had Silly Putty! It was sold in eggs because it was Easter when it was released.

In 1949, Thomas Dam, a Danish fisherman, was financially struggling to get Christmas gifts for his daughter. He decided to make an assortment of dolls for her. He used sheep's wool for the hair, and the

Troll doll was born! They snowballed in popularity. They were initially called Dam Dolls.

Tip 62: Firsts for Toy Collectors

There are a vast amount of toys to satisfy all toy collectors, whether it is one type of toy (cars, dolls, Legos, etc.), or if the collection focuses on a favorite decade. Focus on a decade or if toys just fill up your mixture of collectibles. No one knows who made the first toy, but we are pretty sure it was a curious child with a stick. Some of today's toys were played with by children in the Ancient Greeks, Egyptians, and Romans. Those toys that are still popular today are marbles, stuffed animals, dolls, puppets, kites, playing cards, rocking horses, Dominoes, Checkers, and Chess.

A clockmaker made the Jack-in-the-Box in the 1500s. It was a gift for a local prince. Many do not think of the 1600s when they study the history of toys, but several toys that out-stood the test of time were introduced in that time period. Those toys include Bubbles, Alphabet Blocks (1693). The Dutch brought jump ropes to America in the late 1600s. This is why using two jump ropes is called "Double Dutch." The jigsaw puzzle was created in 1760 by a British mapmaker.

The First Roller Skates were made in 1735 and were a pair of skates attached to shoes. They were the idea of John Joseph Merlin. He first showed off his invention at a party. While showing how they work, he lost control and crashed into a mirror. He patented roller skates in 1760.

Tip 63: Toy Collectibles of the 1800s

The 1800s ushered in a new line of popular toys that would be loved for children for decades. When the rubber duck was invented, it did not float and was solid. Baby Dolls were made in the 1800s. It gave children a chance to pretend to be mom and dad. Before that, dolls resembled miniature adults. Raggedy Ann and Andy were introduced in 1915.

Karl von Drais invented the concept of the bicycle. It was Kirkpatrick Macmillan who added pedals to the bike in 1839. Daniel Carpenter brought us the sled on September 20, 1839. Binney and Smith first made crayons in 1885.

The dollhouse was introduced as a toy in the 1800s. They date back to the 1600s when they were called cabinet houses and were used to display wealth. By the late 1600s, they were used as teaching tools to show little girls the proper way to run a household. They were first called dollhouses in the 1700s and were made to be exact replicas of the owner's home.

Tip 64: Facts of Toy Collectibles 1900 - 1940

The first half of the 1900s brought us the Tinkertoys (1913), Radio Flyer Wagon (1917), and the View Master (1939). Erector Sets were introduced in 1911 and discontinued in 1980.

The classic story of the teddy bear dates back to November 1902 and details a hunting trip that President Theodore Roosevelt participated in with Mississippi Governor Andrew Longino. And a few others. Near the end of the journey, most of the hunters already killed an animal, but Roosevelt did not. A few of the hunters chased a black bear and clubbed it to stop the animal from running. After they tied the bear to a willow tree, they called Roosevelt over to shoot it. He refused, calling it unsportsmanlike. However, he did tell them to shoot the bear to put the animal out of its misery. When political cartoonist Clifford Berryman heard of the incident, he decided to poke fun of it. On November 16, 1902, they released a cartoon image of a bear tied to a tree and a disgusted Roosevelt waving them off. Others mocked the cartoon but made the bear smaller and smaller until it was a cub. When Morris Michtom saw the cartoon, he made a stuffed bear to sell at his shop and named it "Teddy's Bear." They were a huge success, and Michtom opened the Ideal Novelty and Toy Co. At the same time, Richard Steiff was making similar bears. The Steiff Bears are recognizable by the button in their ear and their movable arms and legs,

Edwin Binney left Binney & Smith and started making Crayola Crayons on June 10, 1903. The decade ended with a bang when, in 1900, the first Lionel train was invented, the Electric Express. It was first made as a store display.

When John Lloyd Wright created Lincoln Logs in 1924, he named them after Abraham Lincoln's childhood log home. Toy soldiers were first made in the early 1900s and were metal. The plastic little green army men were introduced in the 1930s.

Tip 65: Fifty Years of Toy Collectibles (1950 - 2000)

Some of the highlighted toys of those years are Play-Doh (1956), the Etch-a-Sketch (1959), and the Easy Bake Oven (1963). GI. Joe was created by Hasbro in 1964 and is considered to be the first action figure. In 1959, Ruth Handler got the idea for the Barbie doll after she watched her daughter playing with paper dolls. Barbie's "official birthday" is March 9, 1959. She developed Barbie's look from the German doll, Bild Lilli, that was introduced on August 12, 1955.

The Frisbee has an exciting history. The idea developed in 1871 with the Frisbie Pie Company. Local college students used to fly the pans to each other and shout "Frisbie" each time. In 1948, Walter Frederick Morrison and Warren Franscioni invented a plastic version of the pan. It was a similar disc shape and named the "Flying Saucer." In 1955, Morrison renamed the toy the Pluto Platter and sold it to the Wham-O Toy Company, who released it in 1957. A year later, they renamed it "Frisbee," a play of words from the pie company's tins but spelled differently to skate around copyright laws.

Hoops have been popular toys for centuries. They were made from bamboo, grapevines, and rattan. The modern Hula Hoop was developed in 1958 by Arthur K. "Spud" Melin and Richard Knerr. They named it after the Hawaiian dance, which mimics the same motions of the hip.

There are several types of collectible toy cars. The earliest toy cars were made by TootsieToy in 1909. Corgi cars were made from 1934-1979. Matchbox cars were introduced in 1954. Their biggest competitor is Hot Wheels, which debuted in 1968. Tonka trucks made construction vehicles. Their first and most famous was the dump truck, which was introduced in 1965. Micro Machines were 1.5 inches long. They were made from 1987-2008. They were brought back in 2015 and discontinued a year later.

Children have always enjoyed playing with dolls. Some of the most sought after dolls by collectors are Tiny Tears (1950), Chatty Cathy (1960), Thumbelina (1961), Mrs. Beasley (1967), Baby Crissy (1973), Cabbage Patch Doll (1978) and Baby Feels So Real (1979).

Collectibles toys of the 1970s include Weebles (1971), the Rubik's Cube, by Erno Rubik, in 1974, Waterful Ring Toss (1976), Stretch Armstrong (1976), the Pet Rock (1976), and Strawberry Shortcake (1979). The Monchhichi was a Japanese monkey who wore a red bib and sucked on his thumb. He was made in 1974. The Smurfs and the Care Bears were introduced in 1981. Polly Pocket debuted in 1983. A year later,

Rainbow Brite and Pound Puppies were created. American Girl Dolls and My Little Ponies were first sold in 1986.

The 1990s brought us a new line of collectible toys, several of which soared in value. Beanie Babies debuted in 1993 and skyrocketed in popularity. The first Ty Beanies were Brownie (Bear) and Pinchers (Lobster). Tamagotchi, the handheld digital pet, was introduced in 1996 and has tripled in value. Pogs were introduced in the United States in 1996. The game was first played in 1920, in Hawaii, and was called Milk Caps. More collectible toys that debuted in the 90s were Super Soakers in 1990, Sky Dancers in 1994, and both Furby and Betty Spaghetty debuted in 1998.

Tip 66: Why We Owe Today's Board Games to Abraham Lincoln

Milton Bradley made the first modern board games in the 1860s. He first opened a lithography shop in Springfield, Massachusetts, in 1860. Bradley was printing colored lithographs of Abraham Lincoln. It was at this time when 11-year-old Grace Bidel, from Westfield, New York, wrote a letter to Lincoln and told him that he should grow a beard because women love whiskers, so he did. Bradley was not sure what to do with all the lithographs he just made that featured a clean-shaven Lincoln. Later that week, during a visit to his friend, George Tapley, they played a game that Bradley thought was boring. So he decided to make his own and named the board game the Checkered Game of Life (it had a suicide square). Bradley made the game on the back of the unusable Lincoln lithograph. They enjoyed the game so much, he created more, using those lithographs of Lincoln that were unusable. On the weekend that he introduced the game, he sold 40,000 copies.

The Civil War started the next day. Bradley pushed his board games aside and decided to sell weapons. Sadly, he saw how bored the soldiers were on their downtime, so he went back to making games. This time, they were small enough to carry in their pockets. The games were chess, checkers, backgammon, dominoes, and "The Checkered Game of Life." He sold them for $1 a piece. The game later became known as "Life."

After the war, he went back to making standard board games. The first two games were "Fire Department" and "Troublesome Pigs." He made them for children because he had just joined the kindergarten movement. The concept of kindergarten was brought to the United States in Elizabeth Peabody in 1860, and Bradley was a strong supporter. It was then that he started the Milton Bradley company. Board games are 18" x 18" because that was the size of the cardboard that would fit inside the lithograph machine.

Tip 67: A Timeline of Collectible Games

Board games started with Chess in the Roman days. The variety of games continues to grow every year.

Here are some of the favorites sought after by collectors.

Yahtzee (1956)

Risk (1957)

Spill and Spell (1957)

Stratego (1963)

Mousetrap (1963)

Twister (April 1966)

Boggle (1972)

Mr. Mouth (1976)

Hungry Hungry Hippo (1978)

Battleship was first played in the 1930s on pen and paper. It was released as a board game in 1967. John Spinello developed the idea of the Operation game in 1964. He sold the game to toy designer Marvin Glass for $500 and the promise of a job upon graduation. He did not follow through with the job offer.

Monopoly was the idea of Elizabeth J. Magie Phillips and was first called the Landlord's Game. She created the game in 1903. For 30 years that followed, many made their own Monopoly games. If you find a handmade Monopoly game, then it is one that was built between 1903-1933. Parker Brothers initially rejected the game. They felt it was too long and had too many rules. After some negotiating, they bought the game in 1933.

When Alfred Butts invented Scrabble in 1931 he originally called the game Criss Cross. In 1948, James Brunot made changes to the game and renamed it Scrabble. It was first sold in England in 1954. Another game to come out of England was "Clue" in 1949. It was the idea of Anthony Pratt.

Chutes and Ladders was introduced in 1943. However, the game's history goes by to Ancient India, in the 13th century when it was called Snakes and Ladders.

Candy Land was created in the early 1940s by Eleanor Abbott to entertain children who were recovering from polio. Abbott was also struck with polio and was in the hospital when she made the game.

The Mystery Date Game was released in 1965. It was so popular with girls that it was reissued in 190, 199, and 2005 to keep up with the styles and times.

The idea of Trivial Pursuit was developed on December 15, 1979, by Chris Haney and Scott Abbott. They were drinking beer while they enjoyed a game of Scrabble when they decided to create their own game.

The 1970s brought on electronic games that have now become collectibles. Simon is one of those games. It was created by Max Baer in 1976. Other handheld electronic games included Mattel's Auto Race (1976), Mattel's Electronic Football (1977), Electronic

Quarterback by Coleco (1978), and Merlin by Parker Brothers (1978).

Ralph H. Baer received the first video game patent and today is known as the Father of Video Games. He received the first video game patent. It was for his system, the Magnavox Odyssey, which was first sold in 1972. Atari also debuted in 1972 with their first game, Pong. The Atari 2600 debuted in 1979. It was the first video game that came with cartridges to allow the player to change games.

Chapter 5: Know the Law

The Legal Side of Collectibles

Under the law, there are several ways for an inventor to protect their discoveries. The most common form of protection is through a patent. Collectors should learn about patents and trademark protections because they reveal the history behind treasured collectibles. When it was invented, by who, and sometimes 'why.'

George Washington made the patent office in 1790. On July 31, 1790, Samuel Hopkins was granted the first patent for a process of making potash (potassium carbonate). This is an ingredient used in fertilizer. An interesting fact about patents is that no one knows who invented the design for the fire hydrant because the patent was burned up in a fire.

Ben Franklin did not patent any of his inventions. He stated, "as we enjoy great advantages from the inventions of others, we should be glad of an opportunity to serve others by any invention of ours and this we should do freely and generously." In 1955, Jonas Salk chose not to patent his polio vaccine for the sake of humanity. If he had patented it, he would have earned an estimated $7 billion.

Tip 68: What to Know about Patents

According to the National Inventor Fraud Center, "a patent is a right granted by the United States to an inventor to exclude others from making, using, selling or importing an invention throughout the United States without the inventor's consent. The inventor may license or sell the rights defined by the claims of the patent." Patents are considered property and can be sold or mortgaged. A day to remember is the "conception date." This was the day that you first had your idea.

If you want to see if someone already has a patent on your idea, you can search for free on the "United States Patent and Trademark Office" website: www.uspto.gov. Be patient! It can take up to three years for the application to finish processing.

Tip 69: The Three Types of Patents

According to the Unites States Patent and Trademark Office, a utility patent protects the way an item is used and works. The duration of the utility patent is for 20 years. The cost is between $5,000-$15,000. However, there are fees that need to be paid during that time.

A "design patent" protects the way an item looks. The cost is between $2,000-$3,500. The patent protects the design for 14 years after the day the application is filed.

A "plant patent" is used to protect the creation of a plant. The cost is between $4,500-$8,000. It expires after 20 years.

Tip 70: How to Apply for a Patent

Patents can only be applied for at the United States Patent and Trademark Office. The process includes a description of the item, detailed drawings, a claim to the product, and an oath. There are two patent applications, the non-provisional patent application, and the provisional patent application.

The provisional patent application is given to an applicant who has an idea for an invention but needs more time to organize the details of the item's mechanics and appearance. They have one year from the day the file to complete a corresponding non-provisional application. After the non-provisional patent application is filed, it can then be examined to see if the idea can receive a patent protection.

Tip 71: The Patent Wars

Some of the history behind patents is often cloaked in heated debates. Alexander Graham Bell and Elisha

Gray fought in court over who was the true inventor of the telephone. The Kellogg Company fought against the National Biscuit Company over the patent rights for shredded wheat cereal. Elias Howe and Isaac Singer fought in court over the true inventor of the sewing machine. Those are some examples.

Glen Curtis invented several aircraft, which included the Red Wing and the White Wing. The designs were pretty similar to that of the Wright Brothers. The dispute ended up in a court battle that lasted four years. It was brutal on both sides. Their lawyers tried to get them to make an amicable agreement, but both sides refused. When Wilbur Wright died in 1912 of typhoid, the family blamed Curtis, citing that worry caused by the lawsuit caused him to lose his health.

Though the movie industry is based in Hollywood on the west coast, it began in New Jersey. However, Thomas Edison was constantly threatening them with lawsuits claiming to have patents on almost everything they tried to do. They were so fed up that they relocated to the other side of the country. They chose California because their Ninth Circuit Court of Appeals was known to rule against patent claims.

Patent wars often brought out the greed in people. The Halliburton Company actually tried to patent patenting. The most disappointing was when Myriad Genetics attempted to patent the breast cancer genes BRCA1 and BRCA2. Myriad wanted to have full control over the price of diagnostic testing and limit research on breast cancer genes. The Supreme Court ordered their request was invalid.

Tip 72: Should You Have a Certificate of Authenticity

A Certificate of Authenticity is verifiable proof that the item is authentic. It should include the name of the item, previous owner information, and any identifying numbers or details, including the production date, dimensions, and edition number. It should also include the certificate of authenticity seal. Because these certificates can be doctored up on the computer, ask to talk to the person that provided the certificate.

Tip 73: The Difference Between a Copyright and a Trademark

A patent protects the shape of the item, and a copyright protects the intricate design. A copyright protects original work, including literary, dramatic, musical, and artistic works, such as poetry, novels, movies, songs, computer software, and architecture. A trademark protects words, phrases, symbols, or designs identifying the creator and distinguishing them from others. An example would be the checkmark used by Nike. The copyright protects the work as a whole. The trademark protects the company name, logo, and phrases.

Tip 74: Why Medicinal Bottles are Illegal

There are collectibles that are illegal to sell. One of those items, are medicinal bottles. Collectors search for bottles made before 1920 for their shape. They buy bottles after 1920 for the things it may have contained. Though, pharmaceutical bottles can still be found at shows and shops. The DEA can come in and pull the items for sale if they contain anything. This is an act that had been in effect since 1908. However, the DEA never started enforcing it until after the 9/11 Attack on America. The reason they are illegal is because the liquid inside can be explosive. Also, with pharmaceuticals, there can be ingredients that are habit-forming.

Tip 75: Illegal Animal Collectibles

Collectibles known as "Animal Statues" are objects made from the fur and parts of animals that were hunted. If the animal was on the endangered species list or if the item was made after 1970, then it will be destroyed. Though the item cannot be sold, it can be given away or donated. If the object is given away before the property owner dies, they can receive a tax deduction. If the transition occurs after the person dies, the person who receives it has to pay taxes on the item's value. The Marine Mammal Protection Act forbids the sale of items made from polar bears after 1972. It is also illegal to sell items of rhino horn, the grizzly bear, and sea turtle shells. The National

Oceanic Atmospheric Administration bans the sale and import of whale teeth or bone.

Tip 76: The Laws of Ivory

The Marine Mammal Protection Act prevents the sale of walrus ivory on collectibles that were made after 1972. It became illegal to import Asian Ivory products on July 1, 1975, and it was no longer legal to import African Ivory on January 18, 1990.

On July 6, 2016, it became illegal to sell all ivory products in the United States. You can own them, give them away, or inherit them, but you cannot sell it. If you have documents that show the Ivory products were imported before the dates banning it, then be sure to keep them as your records. There are some exceptions to the rules. The ivory is 100 years or older. The ivory can only contribute up to 50% of the value. You have documents that prove the item was shipped into the United States before the banned dates were initiated.

Tip 77: Bird Feathers Can Make Your Collection Illegal

It is illegal to collect or sell feathers, eggs, or nests of birds that are protected under the law. You can be fined just for possessing the bird item since there is no way of knowing if you found the feather or got it by killing the bird. There are over 1,000 birds in the

United States that are protected by the Migratory Bird Treaty Act. A list of the birds can be found on the U.S. Fish and Wildlife Service website (fws.gov). The Bald and Golden Eagle Protection Act states the only people allowed to own an Eagle's feather are Native Americans. The person should be able to prove their American Indian Ancestry, which is enrolled in a federally recognized tribe.

Tip 78: Banned and Illegal Collectibles and Antiques

Animals are not the only items protected under the law. The Archaeological Resources Protection Act of 1979 has banned the sale of Native American artifacts made after 1979. Some of the artifacts cannot even be owned unless it is by a museum. Domestic dog and cat furs are banned from imports and sales. Currently, there is a ban on imports and sales of products made in Iran.

Brazilian Rosewood trees were nearly depleted from excessive harvesting. The wood was used to make guitars, marimbas, chess sets, furniture, trays, and humidors. _Brazilian Rosewood is now protected under_ CITES, a multilateral treaty to protect endangered plants and animals established on July 1, 1975. All items made from _Brazilian Rosewood after July 1975 are now illegal to sell._

Tip 79: Dividing Collectibles and Antiques After Divorce

In most cases, if the couple is unable to come to an agreement on who gains property of antiques and collectibles, the judge can order them to be sold and the proceeds divided. There are some exceptions to this. If the items were bought before the marriage, they are not marital property. If the item was purchased as a gift for just one of them, it is not marital property. If the item was bought by one spouse for the other, it is considered an inter-spousal gift, so it is not marital property. When you go through a divorce, take a detailed inventory of all collectibles, be sure to note when the item was bought and the value.

Chapter 6: Cleaning and Preserving Techniques

- To Clean or Not to Clean

- Cleaning Techniques

- Insuring Your Collectibles

- Proper Way to Store Collectibles

Caring for and Cleaning Antiques and Collectibles

Proper storing and displaying of collectibles is important because if done improperly, it can damage your collectibles. Normal wear and tear is expected on antiques and collectibles. Damage can lower the value of the item. This includes cracks, discoloring, stains, broken pieces, chips, sticky drawers, and original pieces that were replaced. There are several ways that furniture can be cleaned without destroying the. This is not always a guarantee. If you are worried about trying to clean an item yourself, you can contact a professional.

Tip 80: Basic Care Rules

When you have antiques and collectibles, there may come a time that you want to clean them. Here are some basic things to remember. For starters, handle all of the items carefully, especially with glass. The older the glass, the more delicate you should be with it. Some of your objects can be cleaned with glass cleaner. Do not use the type that contains bleach. If you decide to try and clean an item, test it in a small area first, preferably underneath if possible. If you have any concerns, take it to a professional.

Tip 81: What NOT to Do When Cleaning Collectibles

Do not try to repair or paint vintage toys.

Do not refinish furniture that was made before 1830.

Do not repair torn paper or photographs with translucent tape.

Never use rust-remover on china, gold, or platinum. It can cause permanent damage.

Do not put crystal or antique glassware in the dishwasher. This rule also applies to china unless it says "dishwasher safe."

Do not hang ceramic plates on spring-type metal plate hangers. They can scratch the item, as well as put stress on the plate, causing it to crack.

Tip 82: Caring for Wood and Furniture

Wood pieces can be cleaned with furniture polish. Use a cotton swab for the crevices.

Cigar ash can remove wax and rings. Sprinkle the cigar ash and wipe in a circular motion until it is gone.

Toothpaste mixed with mayonnaise can also clean rings off of furniture.

Old wooden furniture often has watermarks. To remove them, create a paste that is a mixture of Vaseline and ashes. Use a cloth to wipe over the mark, moving in a circular motion.

For scratches on the wood, rub it a few times with a walnut then smooth it over with your fingers to remove the scratch.

If you want to restore the appearance of the wood, do not use furniture oil. Beeswax or Minwax can give it a better look without damaging the wood.

Tip 83: Oh, Those Stickers

You can't scrub stickers and should not spray cleaning solution on them. It can destroy the sticker. Swipe it once with a cotton swab to remove any loose dirt.

Peanut Butter or cold cream can remove sticker residue or spilled glue.

For stickers that are peeling, attach double-stick tape underneath. Cut the tape to the size of the sticker and apply it with tweezers.

Tip 84: Tips for Cleaning Vintage Furniture

Direct sunlight can cause damage to the wood and for the fabric to fade.

Do not keep vintage furniture near vents or heat sources, ovens, and fireplaces. The heat can cause shrinking, which can then loosen glue joints, veneers, inlays, and marquetry.

If something spills on the fabric, blot it out right away with a paper towel. Do not wipe it because the stain can spread. Do not use a hairdryer because it can cause shrinking, and the stain will set in.

The drawers on antique furniture have a tendency to start sticking from age. This is due to the shrinking and swelling of the wood. If the drawers are sticking, rub the sides with Ivory soap.

It would be best if you did not clean antique furniture with polish, commercial cleaners, or furniture oil. Wipe it with a damp cloth. If there are spills or stains, then glass cleaner would be a safer option.

Tip 85: Proper Cleaning of Dishes, Marble, and Glassware

To clean the glass chimneypiece of an oil lamp, wipe it delicately with a newspaper.

Stoneware dishes can be cleaned by soaking them in a gallon of water with two denture cleaning tablets. Let them soak for at least 24 hours.

Use only white glue when fixing broken pieces of porcelain, stoneware, or pottery. Use a damp cloth to wipe off excess glue.

Jade, Ivory, and Marble should be cleaned delicately, only by wiping gently with a soft cloth or soft brush. Keep the object out of direct sunlight because it will dry it up.

Weeping glass and archaeological glass should only be cleaned by a professional conservator.

If you use Epoxy to repair broken pieces, avoid putting the item in direct sunlight because it can cause a yellowing where the adhesive was added.

Marble tops can be cleaned by wiping the top with warm water. If you need to, you can add a mild detergent to the water. Be sure to wipe the soap away completely; any leftover soap can turn yellow. If the stain is still there, apply a paste made from powdered whiting and water. It creates a consistency similar to peanut butter. Cover it with plastic wrap and tape the edges down. Let it sit for two days. Wipe it away with a damp cloth.

Tip 86: Caring for Ephemera

Display your paper collectibles in frames behind glass or plexiglass.

To store ephemera, never roll them up, including maps and posters. Store them in polyester bags and lay them flat.

Use a Document Cleaning Pad to remove marks from paper. Never use an eraser.

If there is mold or mildew on books or paper, brush it off with a toothbrush/paintbrush, or soft brush.

Do not repair paper or photographs using transparent tape, instead use Document Repair Tape.

If you want to hang old photographs, attach a piece of plastic to the back. This creates a vapor lock and prevents them from molding.

Wear white cotton gloves when handling delicate items, such as photographs, paper, and paintings. The oils on your hands can damage them.

Tip 87: Invest in These Cleaning Supplies

Plaskolite is good for cleaning plastic and other hard surfaces.

Beaumontage is a mixture of resin, beeswax, and shellac. It is used to fill holes or cracks in wood or metal.

Epoxy is the preferred substance used by antique dealers and collectors for fixing broken pieces of glassware.

Triton X-100 is a mild detergent for cleaning wood. It should be diluted before using.

Vulpex is a safe cleaning solution that can be used on almost every surface, from paper to hardwood.

Orvus is a paste shampoo that is used on a variety of textiles. It is also the chosen solution for cleaning quilts.

There are a variety of items that can be used to wipe and dab collectibles during cleaning. You can use a soft cloth, cheesecloths, cotton balls, paintbrushes, very soft toothbrushes, and even a baby brush. If your collectible has delicate pieces attached, do not use the soft cloth (rag). The fibers can snag on the ornamental pieces. Use a dry paintbrush with soft bristles to dust porcelain, pottery, and glass objects.

Tip 88: Plastic Cleaning Tips

The preferred method to clean plastic is to use a mild detergent with warm water. Plaskolite plastic cleaner can also be applied using a cotton swab or soft cloth.

If there is yellowing on the plastic, it can be cleaned with a paste of baking soda and water. Scrub the yellow stains with a soft toothbrush. Once the yellow is removed, wipe the area with warm water and a mild detergent.

For plastic action figures, let them soak in hot soapy water for 5-10 minutes. Scrub the items with a soft toothbrush. Let them air dry for about 30 minutes, then finish drying them with a cloth.

Tip 89: Protecting and Displaying Autographs

The autographed item should be stored in a display case or airtight container and kept at room temperature. If it is saved in an album, then keep it stored upright, so the ink does not run and do not lay anything on top of it. Keep the item out of sunlight and away from bright lights. It will cause the autograph to fade. If you put it in a frame, do not let the signature touch the glass. The signature will transfer onto the glass.

Tip 90: Creative Ways to Display Small Collectibles

Matchbox cars can be displayed in shadow boxes.

Buttons, brooches, and enamel pins can be stored and displayed on pennants and even pillows.

Hang cookie sheets on the wall to display magnets. To add a splash of color, you can paint the cookie sheets a variety of colors.

Small collectibles, such as marbles, balls, or seashells, can be stores and displayed in vases.

There are albums with sheets to save trading cards. They can also hold other pieces of ephemera, including small photos and business cards.

People prefer to save Barbie Dolls, GI Joes, and action figures in the original packaging. If you come across ones that are missing the box, they can be stored and displayed in shoe bags.

Most people display their collectibles on shelves. When the collection grows so big that it overflows the shelves, you can store the collectibles and later rotate the items. You can also make displays in other rooms. If possible, designate a large area of your home for the collectibles.

Tip 91: What you Should Know About Storing Collectibles

Keep collectibles out of direct sunlight. It can cause colors to fade, wood to shrink, and material to warp.

Storage bins that are air and watertight are the better choices for storing smaller items.

If you have shelves with glass doors, they would be ideal for figurines. It keeps the dust for settling into crevices.

When storing antiques and collectibles, choose an area that is dry, clean, and maintains a consistent temperature. Fluctuating temperatures can damage the items. Try to avoid the attic, basement, or garage. These areas can cause molding and can reach extreme temperatures.

Use acid-free paper between the items to protect them from scratching and deteriorating. Newspapers and regular tissue paper are not acid-free.

Tip 92: Protecting Collectibles and Antiques

Store vintage textiles flat with a minimum number of folds.

Do not wrap breakable items in bubble wrap because the material retains heat.

Do not stack breakables. There is too much of a chance of them falling over and getting damaged.

Before you store vinyl records, clean them thoroughly with a record cleaning brush. Store them in their original jackets and in an upright condition. Records that are stored at a slant can warp over time due to uneven pressure.

If you wrap the collectibles in cloth, only use white. If you use colored cloth, there is a risk of the dye transferring onto the collectible.

Pottery collectibles should be stored on wooden or metal shelves with room between them for air to circulate.

Fragile objects made of glass, pottery or porcelain should never be stacked on top of each other inside a box. The best containers for storing these items are the under-the-bed plastic storage bins.

When you store porcelain dolls, do not put them in airtight containers. The cloth needs to breathe. Wrap the dolls in acid-free paper and store them in small containers.

When storing antique china, wrap them, and store them in containers. The plates and bowls should be placed on their sides.

Tip 93: Insuring Collectibles

You can provide the best care for your collectibles, but still, things happen. Things get broken, fires break out, natural disasters occur, and robberies take place. For all of this, you will need insurance. Unfortunately, only about 30% of the collectors insure their items. Before you can apply for insurance, you need to have your collectibles appraised. There are four types of insurance policies for collectibles and antiques.

A homeowner's insurance with adjusted antiques and collectibles coverage is best if you have a small collection or if you are just starting.

A homeowner's insurance with an antiques and collectibles rider is for collectors with medium-sized collections.

Consider a separate policy for collections that are large in size or include rare and specialized pieces.

Chapter 7: Know How to Buy & Sell

- What to Know About Autographs

- Checking for Authenticity

- Aging Wood in Collectibles

- Tips for Buying and Selling

- Future Collectibles

Know What You Have When It Is Time to Sell

The world of antiques and collectibles holds excitement, mystery, and new discoveries around every corner. It also carries their share of scams and con artists. It is important to know how to detect the fakes from the genuine pieces. Do not be upset with yourself if you fall for a con. It happens to the best of all collectors. This information will teach you a number of ways to protect yourself as you buy, trade, and sell your treasured pieces.

Tip 94: Checking the Authenticity of Autographs

Once in a while, you may find a piece for your collection that is autographed. It will be either the item or the box that is signed. Here are some things to remember about autographs. Not all signatures are legitimate. Some of them were signed by secretaries, assistants, or fan club volunteers. For example, almost all of the Walt Disney autographs were signed by his secretaries. There are a few that are authentic, but not many. However, if you come across his name signed "Walter Disney," that is always him. It is also rare and highly valuable. The best way to check on an autograph's authenticity is to look up the signature on a reputable site and compare the two.

You can find the authentic autograph on websites like Google and eBay and compare the two. It is best to turn them upside-down when you do it. That way, your mind is not just reading the autograph and can pick out the inconsistencies easier.

Hold the autograph up to the light. If the paper lights up the same as the paper, then it was preprinted. If it glows purple or silver, then it is most likely a stamp. Look at the edge of the signature. This is where the age shows. Older autographs have a purple-grey look. Much older photographs will have a brown-yellow look around the edge of the signature caused by the iron in the ink. Run your finger over it. You should be able to feel the texture. Stamped autographs are in black or white. So, if the pen color is blue, red, or even purple, it is not a stamp. Felt tip pens did not exist before the 1960s.

Use a magnifying glass to spot out these tell-tale signs. If it shows hesitations between the letters or equal pressure throughout, then it is most likely a stamp. If there are letters that cross over each other like an "X" or a lowercase "t," you can see which line was drawn first through a magnifying glass.

Tip 95: Simple Tests of Authenticity

To check your crystal, give it the Ping Test. Tap or click the item. If it is real crystal, it will make a pinging sound. Also, wet your finger and run it around the rib of your crystal glass. If it is authentic, it will make a sound similar to a music note.

To tell if an item is real brass, put a magnet against it. The magnet will not stick if it is pure brass.

To determine if items are pure alabaster, hold a flashlight to it. Light will go through and reflect.

Both Custard Glass and Vaseline Glass will glow under a black light.

Bakelite is a popular collectible, and there is a simple way to test the piece for authenticity by using Simichrome polish. It is a creamy polish that will not scratch the metal. Rub a dab of the Simichrome polish on the item in question, either on the side or the bottom. If the cloth used turns yellow, then it is genuine Bakelite.

Often during the making of the crock and pottery, small lumps form before they are placed in the kiln. The glaze later settles over it. There may also be different levels of thickness near the top. These mistakes are natural since they are made by hand and not machines. You may not be able to see them, but you can feel them when you run your hand over it.

Tip 96: Five Things to Look for When Checking for Originality

You can check through touch. Items that are hand-carved are uneven and are not smooth.

The smell can give away the item's age. Newer pieces still have the wood smell. Older items have a musty mildewed smell.

Check what is inside. Synthetic stuffing was not invented until the 1920s. Before that, stuffing consisted of natural materials, such as animal hair or straw.

Look for signs of aging. On a replica, the marks are equal in different locations. This is not the same for an original. For example, if the arms on a chair have the same level of wear as the part where the hands and arms rest, then it is a replica.

What the hardware can tell you. On newer pieces, the hardware all matches. The original pieces used different types of hardware (nails, screws, etc.) because they were harder to obtain. Remember, the

Phillip's screw was not invented until 1933. Older pieces used single-slot screws and square nails. Originals also often used different styles of wood. The less expensive wood was used under chairs and inside the drawers because no one was going to see it anyway. So, when you see the different styles of wood, it is an original. Dovetail joints was a technique often used in older pieces. Fibreboards and staples always indicate a replica.

Tip 97: Know the Signs of Dovetailing

Another way to detect vintage wooden furniture from a replica is to look for signs of aging in the dovetailing. When two pieces of wood are brought together to fit like pieces in a puzzle, the process is called dovetailing. A wooden drawer that shows no signs of dovetail joints is not as old as you think. When you do spot dovetails on furniture, remember that happens as the item ages. The older the item, the larger the dovetails will be, and the farther apart they will appear.

Tip 98: A Secret to Wooden Collectibles

Wood shrinks as it ages. Any piece over 100 years old will show shrinkage going across the grain. If it does not have that appearance, then it is not as old as you think it is. Wood separation happens around the edge of cabinet doors and in the drawers. When you pull the drawer out, you will notice that the bottom panel is separated along the edge. This happens when the wood shrinks from age. This does not depreciate the value; it is accepted as a part of the furniture's history.

If you are buying a collectible that is made of wood, feel around the edge. As timber gets older, it softens, especially at the 100-year mark. If it feels firm and sharp, then it was either restored (which decreases the value), or it is not as old as they say it is. One of the oldest manufacturers of wooden products and furniture is Chippendale. It should always be soft to the touch.

Tip 99: A Checklist for Buyers and Sellers

Keep a record of all items that you sell, including all information that was provided to the buyer.

Obtain a receipt for all purchases. It should include the name and address of the seller.

Ask for a written provenance that establishes the item's descriptions. This should always be put in writing, no verbal agreements.

If the item has been repaired or restored, all of the details on that should be put in writing.

If the item is sold with a Certificate of Authenticity, explain how it was examined that makes the certificate authentic.

Make sure that the information for each item for sale has been recorded accurately. If you have staff, they should be aware of the information as well. This is needed when asked by the buyer to "tell me something about this."

There should be a fair and honest marketplace for antiques and collectibles. The buyer should be comfortable asking questions when they are in doubt and, in return, must always be given truthful answers.

Tip 100: Should You Haggle on the Price

It is okay to haggle on a price if you are at a yard sale, thrift store, or buying from someone through an ad. If you are at an auction, antique store, or buying from another collector, then you will not be in a position to ask for a lower price. These people have put work into preserving the item and have overhead costs to cover.

The patent office can help you deduce the age of an antique toy. There is a small fee required, but they can also provide the toymaker and the date the patent was filed. Send this information to their office.

Check the Patent
Maker's Mark
Country of Origin
Any Patent Numbers on the Toy

Tip 101: Rules of the Consumer Protection Regulation

The Consumer Protection Regulation (CPR) prohibits commercial practices that are deemed unfair. They monitor the actions of traders to keep them from using information that is false or misleading. They also cannot omit information that a buyer needs to make an informed decision. These are basic regulations set by the CPR's.

Provide information on what the product actually is.

Explain the composition of the item (what it is made of).

Detail the geographical origin of where the item was created.

Provide the method and date it was manufactured (making it older than it is).

Give all information on what it was used for previously.

Explain the price that was paid for the item and the value today.

Whether the item can be bought at a different price or location (stating it is rare if it is not).

Tip 102: Resources to Guide Collectors Away from the Fakes

There are websites that instruct on ways to distinguish frauds from the genuine pieces.

Railroadiana Online (railroadiana.org) – They list a number of fakes that have been growing in the area of railroad pieces and memorabilia.

Clock History (clockhistory.com) – Filled with information on fake clocks being produced.

Wagner and Griswold Society (griswoldandwagner.com) - A history of fake Griswold cast iron skillets.

Drexel Grapevine Antiques (drexelantiques.com) – They display hunting and fishing badges and explain the details. This will help collectors tell the fakes from the reproductions.

Reproduction of Antique Bottles (antiquebottles.com) – This is an excellent resource for bottle collectors checking the authenticity of their collectible.

McCoy Pottery Collectors Society (mccoypotterycollectorssociety.com) – McCoy pieces are among the most collected pieces of pottery. This website gives great details of the fakes that have plagued the collectible world.

Tip 103: Time to Buy – And Sell!

When you decide to sell your collectibles, there are several ways to do this. Learn the value of the item before you arrange any sales. You can do this by taking the item to an appraiser or antique dealer. There is another way that you can do this yourself, using the internet. Compare the piece to what others are selling their collectible for online. Here are ten websites where you can do that.

eBay	Bonanza
Etsy	Market Stall
Mercari	Online Forums
Craigslist	Flea Market
Amazon	Hobby Shop
Facebook	Consignment Shop

You can sell your collectibles in-person to antique dealers, fellow collectors, antique malls, and auction houses. If you want to sell the pieces online, you can go back and use the web sites eBay, Etsy, Mercari, Amazon, Facebook, and Bonanza. These are more ways to also sell your collectibles online.

TIAS is the oldest antique mall on the Web.

Ruby Lane is one of the world's largest marketplaces for antiques and collectibles.

Heritage Auctions is an auction website to buy and sell antiques and collectibles.

"Antiques and Collectibles Buyers" is an Instagram group that buys and sells a variety of pieces.

When it comes to buying collectibles, whether it is online or in person, remember - "Caveat Emptor," which is Latin for "let the buyer beware."

Tip 104: Household Collectibles Rising in Value

Kitchen and Household antiques have always been among the favorites in the collectibles community. There are some new collectibles that have been added to the list through the years.

Farm Tables	Persian Rugs
Lamps	China Sets
Silverware	Furniture
Barware	Perfume Bottles
Pyrex	Depression Glass
Silver Flatware	Hubley Cast-Iron Doorsteps
Cereal Boxes	Artwork (Funky Art and Equestrian Art)

Tip 105: Toy Collectibles of the Future

We can never predict which toys will increase in value. We can only guess. This is an updated list of some of the most sought after toy collectibles today.

80s Toys	Original Star Wars figures
Sports Cards	Anything Polly Pocket

Pokemon Cards	Electronic Games
Porcelain Dolls	Dollhouses
Comic Books	Ty Beanies (with the tags)
Star Trek	Lionel Train Sets
American Girl Dolls	Milton Bradley Board Games

In the 1990's everyone was positive that those adorable beanie babies would skyrocket in value, and though some have, many are only valued at a few dollars. These items are considered future collectibles.

Shoot Cows is almost certain to be a sought-after card game among collectors. It is described as a "survival horror comedy card game." Since it's introduction, it has grown in popularity, proving that Shoot Cows will one day earn a spot in the collectibles community between Garbage Pail Kids and Pokemon.

Imaginext are figures based on characters from TV, movies, and comic books.

Just as Star Wars and Star Trek figures rose in value, it is predicted that the same will happen with Skylanders, Fortnight, Harry Potter, and The Simpsons.

TeenyMates are one-inch tall figures of sports teams and the WWE wrestlers.

Tsum Tsums are rectangular-shaped character toys. The word "tsum" means "to stack in Japanese.

Limited Edition Lego sets are on the list. If you plan to resell them, do not assemble the kits. Or you can do both, and buy two kits – one to build and one to keep in the box, untouched.

Limited Edition Boards Games are here on the list because collectors love to hear the words "limited edition." Clue, Trivial Pursuit, and Monopoly made several of these games.

Playmobil has been making playsets since 1958. They started with a racecar and grew to make airplanes, airports, buses, campers, and more. Those sets have increased in value. The new ones of today are believed to continue in that same way.

The best advice is to maintain the items in its original condition, with the instructions and extra pieces. Then wait to see what happens. If the collectible does not increase in value, you will still have the fun of having it in your collection. Today's curious treasure hunters are tomorrow's Supercollectors!

Chapter 8: Know Your Collectibles Community

- Categories of Collectibles

- Collectible Museums Across the Country

- Virtual Museums

- Landmark Homes You Can Tour

- Meet Your Peers (Clubs and Organizations)

The Collectibles Community

The collector's community is a vast field of people with one thing in common; they have each found a passion for a particular item. They enjoy comparing adventures, swapping ideas, and sharing the detailed history of their treasured collections. In this community are collectors looking for bee pins, Avon perfume bottles, vintage hats, classic cars, and so much more. It is a big beautiful world that once you join, you will only want to grow from there.

Tip 106: Find Your Collectible Niche

This is a list of collectible categories and a few examples of sought-after pieces that are looked for by individuals. Some focus on just one item in the genre, where others collect a variety of those pieces. This will help you understand the different groups. You may just find a whole new collection to start.

General Collectibles: Artwork, Science-Fiction (UFO, Aliens), Soakies (bubble bath bottles), Rubber Ducks, Pirates, Favorite Animal, Ladybug, Butterfly, Dragonfly, Holiday, Pagers, Campaign Items, Americana, Cameras, Pagers

Breweriana: Beer Cans, Beer Bottles, Cocktail Shakers, Shot Glasses, Decanters, Bar Signs, Cocktail Stirs, Ads, Labels, Beer Mugs, Coasters, Corkscrews, Brewery or Brand Names

Military: Trench Art, Medals, Uncle Sam, V-Mail, Pin-Ups, Dog Tags, Military Patches, Homefront Posters, Submarines

Bank Notes and Coins: Coins, Bank Notes, Tokens, Medals, Wooden Nickels

Entertainment: TV, Movies, Music, Theatre, Magic Memorabilia, Carnivals, Amusement Parks, World's Fair, Carousels, Circus, Souvenirs, Artifacts, Performers, Programs, Clowns

Advertisements/Signs: Soap Ads, Thermometers, Art, Ashtrays, Labels, Clocks, Characters, TV Station Premiums

Ephemera: All Paper Items, Paper Dolls, Greeting Cards, Newspapers, Magazines, Tickets, Posters, Calendars, Folders, Menus, Maps, Books, Stationery, Sheet Music, Photograph

Memorable Moments: Women's Movement, Old Schoolhouse, Halley's Comet, Moon Landing, Titanic

Tobacco: Cigarette Company, Cigarette Packs, Cigarette Cases, Lighters, Ashtrays, Pipes, Cigars, Cigar Boxes, Humidors

Mystical: Fairy, Unicorn, Gnome, Pegasus, Astrology, Tarot Cards, Lucky Charms, Mermaid, Gargoyle, Health Balls, Ouija

Outdoor Categories

Wilderness Sports: Fishing, Hunting, Camping, Fishing Poles, Flashlights, Canteens, Walking Sticks, Firearms, Flashlight, Lantern, Thermos, Compass, Pocketknife

Sports: Favorite Sport, Harlem Globetrotters, Olympics, Pennants, Jerseys, Caps, Trading Cards, Board Games, Autographs, Helmets, Skis, Snowmobiles

Ocean: Windmills, Fish and Sea Life, Oyster Plates, Sea Shells, Sand Dollars, Oyster Shells, Sharks, Whales, Dolphins, Seals, Beach Towels, Beach Safe Containers

Transportation: Airplanes, Helicopters, Blimps, Hot Air Balloons, Airline Memorabilia, Trains, Taxi Cabs, Buses, Automobiles

Botany and Gardening: Flowers, Seeds, Gardening Tools, Water Cans, Lawn Ornaments, Lawn Stones, Wind Chimes, Wind Socks, Bird Baths, Leaves

Landmarks and Architecture: Statue of Liberty, National Parks, Niagara Falls, Route 66, Mount Rushmore, Yosemite, Yellowstone, Empire State Building, Skyscrapers, Eiffel Tower, Windmills, Lighthouse

Occupation and Lifestyle Categories

Gas Station - Gas Station Premiums, Gas Pumps, Signs

Barbershop - Barbershop Memorabilia, Shaving Mugs

Farming: Tractors, John Deere, Barns, Scarecrows, Farm Sets

Firefighting: Fire Hall Memorabilia, Firetrucks, Uniform Patches, Fire Trucks

Banking and Insurance Companies: Banking Items, Checks, Insurance Companies, Fire Marks, Safes

General Store: Coin-Op Machines, Cash Registers, Signs, Store Supplies, Gumball Machines, Candy Jar

Religion: Churches, Crosses, Bibles, Angels, Noah's Ark, Amish, WWJD, Cherubs

Writer: Paperweights, Pens and Pencils, Stationery, Typewriters, Ink Wells, Desk Lamps, Pen Cups, Clipboards, Magnetic Sculptures, Staplers, Letter Openers

Medical: Doctor & Dentist Pieces, Nurse Items, Ambulances, Medicine Jars, Band-Aids, Medicine Tins, Pill Bottles, Apothecary Jars, Pill Boxes

Organizations: Freemasons, Red Cross, Salvation Army, Red Hat Society, Boy Scouts, Girl Scouts, American Legion, Moose Lodge, The Elks

Science: Astronomy, Chemistry Sets, Beakers, Telescopes, Stars, Celestial, NASA, Charles Darwin, Weather Vanes, Barometers, Dinosaurs, Rocks, Fossils

Post Office: Stamps, Mailboxes, Stamp Dispensers, Post Office Memorabilia

Law Enforcement: Badges, Police Station Memorabilia, Police Cars, Uniform Patches

Mining and Blacksmith: Silver Mines, Gold Mines, Blacksmiths, Coal Mines, Oil Mines

Occupation and Business: Truck Driver, Farming, General Store

Diners and Fast Food Restaurants: Sugar Packets, Menus, Diner Supplies and Memorabilia, Dishes, Restaurant Memorabilia

Toy Categories

Toy Styles: Antique Toys, Tin Toys, Wind-Up Toys, Wooden Toys, Remote Control Toys, Battery Operated Toys

Crafts: Art Sets, Crayola, Coloring Books, Paint Books, Stencils, Stickers, Gel Pens

Toys (Stuffed): Beanies, Calico Critters, Sock Monkeys, Teddy Bears

Games: Marbles, Board Games, Card Games, Puzzles, BINGO, Dice, Playing Cards, Pogs (Milk Caps), Darts, Pinball Machines

Toys: Stoves, Trains, Puppets, Dollhouses, Eight Balls, Yo-Yo's, Action Figures, Guns, Telephones, Play Money, Tops and Gyroscopes, Military, Record Player, Play-Doh

Cars & Trucks: Tonka Trucks, Matchbox, Hot Wheels, Micro Machines, Remote Control Cars, Finger Bikes, Penny Racers, Corgi, TootsieToy

Toy Sets: Weebles Sets, Playmobil Sets, Candy Makers, Easy Bake Ovens, Littlest Pet Shop, LEGOS, Erector Sets, Tinkertoys, Polly Pocket

Outside and Ride-On Toys: Kites, Frisbee, Sleds, Ice Skates, Roller Skates, Skateboards, Bicycles, Pedal Cars, Scooter, Rocking Horse, Wagons

Dolls: Trolls, Holly Hobbie, Bratz, Raggedy Ann & Andy, Barbie, Cabbage Patch, Pop Culture, Rainbow

Brite, Kewpies, Indian, Ceramic Dolls, Porcelain Dolls, Bisque Dolls, Marionettes,

Cartoons: Disney, Care Bears, Speed Racer, My Little Pony, Strawberry Shortcake, Casper, Scooby-Doo, Simpsons, Loony Tunes, Smurfs, Popeye, Sailor Moon, Yogi Bear, Pound Puppies

Sunday Comics and Cartoon Characters: Beetle Baily, Garfield, Family Circus, Peanuts, Funny Bunny, Hello Kitty, Lisa Frank

Robots and Electronics: Robots, Video Games and Systems, Hand Held Games, Game Characters, Poo-Chi, Giga Pets, Furby

Super Heroes: Superman, Batman, Spiderman, Flash, Aquaman, Wonder Woman, Teenage Mutant Ninja Turtles, Power Rangers, VR Troopers, Avengers, Incredible Hulk

Home & Decor Categories

Glassware: Dishes (sets), Crocks, Wine Glass, Shot Glass, Carafe, Pitchers, Goblets, Beer Mugs, Drinking Sets, Style of Glassware (listed in chapter 3)

Trinkets: Bells, Miniatures, Candles, Banks, Vase, Head Vase, Eggs, Nesting Doll, Hinged Box, Nodders, Spoons, Smiley Faces, Yin Yangs, Lighthouse, Paperweights

Figurines: Beer Steins, Precious Moments, Cherished Teddies, Snow Babies, Willow Tree, Kelvin's, Hummel, Napco, Paula Statues, Josef Originals, Funko Pop, Lladro, Charming Tails

Fashion: Jeans, T-Shirts, Shoes, Hats, Hat Boxes, Hat Pins, Iron-On Transfers, Belts & Buckles, Ties, Bandannas, Hand Fans, Hand Bags, Gloves, Cuff Links, Tie Clips, Parasols

Vanity and Jewelry: Vanity Trays, Bakelite, Compacts, Powder Jars, Charms, Lockets, Cameos, Manicure Sets, Mirrors, Comb & Brush Sets, Indian Jewelry, Grunge Jewelry

Kitchen: Napkin Rings, Cookie Cutters, Creamers, Salt & Pepper Shakers, Pepper Grinders, Salts, Cruets, Sugar Shakers, Egg Cups, Cookie Jars, Rolling Pins, Antique Appliances Magnets

Food, Snacks, Candy: Cereal Boxes, Specific Food or Snack (Tomato, Strawberry, Apple, Potato Chips, Popcorn, Hot Dogs), Food Labels, Hershey, Bubble Gum, PEZ

Beverages: Milk Bottles, Hot Chocolate, Tea, Coffee, Soft Drinks, Tang, Kool-Aid, Yoo Hoo

Country: Gingerbread Man, Baskets, Apple Crates, Bird Houses, Bird Cages, Buckets, Butter Churns, Quilts, Canning Jars, Jugs, Jars and Jardinieres, Washboards, Saltbox Houses

Hardware: Tools, Switch Plates, Locks, Keys, Mailboxes, Doorknobs, Door knockers, Tiles, Flue Covers

Furniture and Household - Chairs, Tables, Shelves, Vacuums, Washing Machines, Lamps, Irons, Laundry Sprinkler Bottles, Toasters, Sewing Machines

Sewing: Thimbles, Pin Cushions, Beads, Petite Point, Needle Point, Cross Stitch, Plastic Canvas, Sewing Kits, Patches, String Holders, Sewing Clamps, Patterns

Timepieces: Clocks, Cuckoo Clock, Watches, Disney Watches, Character Watches, Swatch

Tip 107: Learn About the World of Museums

Museology is known as the history of museums and their role in society. According to the Institute of Museum and Library Services (IMLS), there are 35,144 museums in the United States. Due to museums opening and closing periodically, the number changes each year. The first museum was built in 1683 on Beaumont Street in Oxford, England. This was the Ashmolean Museum of Art and Archaeology and was a part of Oxford University.

There are some categories of museums that can be found in all 50 states in America. For example, the first museum built to showcase Circus memorabilia was the Circus World Museum in Baraboo, Wisconsin.

It opened in 1884. Today there are circus museums across the country. Other types of museums that have been peppered across America are vintage mansions and log cabins, dating back to the 1700s, that now showcase life in that time period. These museum types can also be found in each state.

Art	Printing
Mining	Bicycle
Music	Glassware
Sports	Tools
Military	Clocks
History	Automobiles
Railroad	Motorcycles
Science	Civil Rights
Aviation	Religious
Maritime	Firefighters
Medical	Law Enforcement
Schoolhouse	General Store
Dinosaurs	Native American
Photography	Old West/Wild West
Farming & Dairy	Toys and Dolls
African American	Telephone
Trolley	Scouting

Virtual Museums

There are now virtual museums! Collectors can delve into the history of antiques and collectibles and explore museums worldwide, from their comfy couch at home! These are just a few virtual museums today.

Toaster Museum (toastermuseum.com)

The Beer Museum (thebeermuseum.com)

Museum of Failure (museumoffailure.com)

The Glass Museum (theglassmuseum.com)

Museum of Failure (museumoffailure.com)

The Anne Frank House (annefrank.org/en)

Flying Disc Museum (Flyingdiscmuseum.com)

Museum of Broken Relationships (brokenships.com)

Moist Towelette Online Museum
(moisttowelettemuseum.com)

Crispus Attucks Online Museum
(crispusattucksmuseum.org)

Virtual Apple Parer Museum
(appleparermuseum.com)

The Disability History Museum
(disabilitymuseum.org)

Virtual Museum of Historical Bottles and Glasses
(fohbcvirtualmuseum.org)

US Navy Poster Museum
(Facebook.com/USNAVYPOSTERMUSEUM)

Unique Museums

Among the popular museums are the odd & quirky, but just as fun, collectible and antique museums. One even brags about its unusual collection in their name - Museum of the Weird (Austin, Texas). The Mel Fisher's Treasure Museum has a collection of treasures that were salvaged from wrecked ships. Inside the Rivermarket Antique Mall is the Lunchbox Musem, home of the world's largest collection of lunchboxes. The museum has been featured on Roadside America and the Food Network.

The Bayernhof Music Museum is a vast collection of music boxes and music machines. Here are more unique museums that also boast the odd, the fun, and the most unforgettable collectibles of yesterday and today. The J.M. Davis Arms and Historical Museum has a remarkable exhibition of over 20,000 guns and a collection of knives.

The Ice House Museum is located in Cedar Falls, Iowa, that was home to an ice house business, in 1858. Ice Houses came and went until November 1921, when the Cedar Falls Ice and Fuel Company erected the building that stands today. In 1976, the ice house had long been closed, and the building stood vacant, teetering on demolition. These are even more unique museums in America.

The Angel Museum (Beloit, Wisconsin)

Steins Unlimited (Pamplin, Virginia)

Merry-Go-Round Museum (Sandusky, Ohio)

Neon Museums (Las Vegas, Nevada)

Kazoo Museum (Eden, New York)

Museum of the Bible (Washington, D.C.)

The Museum of the Weird (Austin, Texas)

Money Museum (Colorado Springs, Colorado)

Umbrella Cover Museum (Peaks Island, Maine)

Mothman Museum (Point Pleasant, West Virginia)

Devils Rope Barbed Wire Museum (McLean, Texas)

ESSE Purse Museum and Store (Little Rock, Arkansas)

The Museum of disABILITY History (Buffalo, New York)

Museum of Miniature Houses (Carmel, Indiana)

American Banjo Museum (Oklahoma City, Oklahoma)

Sila Lydia Bast Bell Museum (Germantown, Wisconsin)

Leland Ms Birthplace of Kermit the Frog (Leland, Mississippi)

Rhode Island Computer Museum (North Kingstown, Rhode Island)

American Celebration on Parade (Shenandoah Caverns, Virginia)

Witch's Dungeon Classic Movie Museum (Bristol, Connecticut)

Art Museums

Daniel Wadsworth founded the Wadsworth Atheneum Museum of Art in 1842. It is considered to be the oldest museum in America. Today it is home to over 50,000 pieces of artwork that span over a period of 5,000 years. Among the art museums that showcase paintings and sculptures are bold and funky museums that delight visitors with one-of-a-kind artwork.

Match Stick Marvels, in Gladbrook, Iowa, is a museum with scaled models of lifelike sculptures, intricate machines, and world-renown architecture made from matchsticks.

The Museum of Bad Art is exactly that - a collection of ugly art. They are located in the basement of the Somerville Theater in Davis Square, Somerville, Massachusetts. They describe their collection of over 700 pieces as "art too bad to be ignored."

Leila's Hair Museum, in Independence, Missouri, displays a collection of wreaths intricately crafted from hair. Some of the hair dates back to 1956. When you visit the museum, check out the glass cases housing a collection of hair jewelry.

The Toilet Seat Museum found at Alamo Heights, Texas, features artwork that has been painted on a collection of toilet seats. Barney Smith collected over 1,400 pieces, making the Toilet Seat Museum a unique part of art history.

The Museum of Pizza flaunts an array of artwork that celebrates the hot cheesy dish of pizza. Guests are even served a slice of pizza while they explore the museum. The museum located on Wythe Avenue in New York takes on a new look at what art brings to the world.

Museums for Figurines and Glassware

There are two types of Glassware collectors. The first is those who collect items made of glass, such as Lladro. The second, are those who prefer a specific type of glass, such as Fiestaware. And there are museums dedicated to making them all happy. The Evelyn Burrow Museum houses everything "Glassware." Then there is the Bergstrom-Mahler Museum of Glass, dedicated to paperweights. These museums also share a variety of glassware collectibles with a long and rich history.

Corning Museum of Glass (Corning, New York)

Fostoria Glass Museum (Moundsville, West Virginia)

National Heisey Glass Museum (Newark, Ohio)

American Toby Jug Museum (Evanston, Illinois)

Fenton Art Glass Museum (Williamstown, West Virginia)

Duncan & Miller Glass Museum (Washington, Pennsylvania)

Sports Museums

When you think of Sports Museums, this is what comes to mind: baseball, football, basketball, hockey...and maybe soccer. There is more than that for sports enthusiasts. The National Freshwater Fishing Hall of Fame & Museum displays over 40 mounted fish. Colorado Springs, Colorado, is home to the ProRodeo Hall of Fame and Museum of the American Cowboy. Here are a few sports museums that you may not know about – but will enjoy just as much.

History of Diving Museum (Islamorada, Florida)

Man in the Sea Museum (Panama City, Florida)

Muhammad Ali Center (Louisville, Kentucky)

The International Bowling Museum (Arlington, Texas)

Mammoth Ski Museum (Mammoth Lakes, California)

World Figure Skating Museum and Hall of Fame (Colorado Springs, Colorado)

Pendleton Round-Up and Happy Canyon Hall of Fame (Pendleton, Oregon)

International Swimming Hall of Fame and Museum (Fort Lauderdale, Florida)

Museums for Outdoor Activities & Recreational Sports

Museums dedicated to outdoor activities and recreational sports include Bicycle Heaven, home to 30,000 vintage and music bicycles, and the Discovery Shell Museum. Visitors can view over 10,000 different seashells from all around the world. If you like the seashell museum, you will adore the Ocean City Life-Saving Station Museum. There is a display of sands, which are also from around the world. The Snowmobile Barn Museum includes over 300 sleds. Collectors will also find these museums interesting.

California Surf Museum (Oceanside, California)

Houston Bicycle Museum (Houston, Texas)

Shattuck Windmill Museum (Shattuck, Oklahoma)

Museum of Yachting (Newport, Rhode Island)

Louisville Slugger Museum & Factory (Louisville, Kentucky)

National Museum of Roller Skating (Lincoln, Nebraska)

Skateboarding Hall of Fame and Museum (Simi Valley, California)

Wisconsin Canoe Heritage Museum (Spooner, Wisconsin)

National Balloon Museum and Ballooning Hall of Fame (Indianola, Indiana)

Little Congress Bicycle Museums (Cumberland Gap, Tennessee)

Transportation Museums

There are museums across America dedicated to showcasing the history of automobiles. Still, some are devoted to a specific vehicle and a few more that stand out in that area. The Elwood Haynes Museum is dedicated to Haynes, the man who was the first to produce cars commercially in 1894. He also discovered stainless steel. The Coolspring Power Museum contains 250 internal combustion stationary gas engines. The International Towing and Recovery Hall of Fame and Museum can be found in Chatanooga, Tennessee. Here are just a few of those for transportation collectors to enjoy.

Buggy Barn Museum (Blanco, Texas)

Caboose Museum (Hermann, Missouri)

National Packard Museum (Warren, Ohio)

Horse and Buggy Museum (Biggsville, Illinois)

Harley-Davidson Museum (Milwaukee, Wisconsin)

Afton Station Packard Museum (Afton, Oklahoma)

National Corvette Museum (Bowling Green, Kentucky)

National Helicopter Museum (Stratford, Connecticut)

Mack Trucks Historical Museum (Allentown, Pennsylvania)

Rocky Mountain Motorcycle Museum (Colorado Springs, Colorado)

Mercedes-Benz Visitor Center and Museum (Vance, Alabama)

Museums for Hobby and Entertainment Collectors

The Star Worlds Arcade exhibits a collection of 80's video games. Nestled in the city of Pittsburgh is Photo Antiquities Museum of Photographic History. The museum boasts an impressive array of photographic history that includes daguerrotypes, tintypes, over 500,000 vintage photographs, over 2,000 cameras, and more! If your collection focuses on a beloved hobby, then these museums are just the right places for you to visit.

National Hobo Museum (Britt, Iowa)

Silverball Museum (Delray Beach, Florida)

Chicago Billiard Museum (Chicago, Illinois)

Logic Puzzle Museum (Burlington, Wisconsin)

Houdini Museum (Scranton, Pennsylvania)

Nevada Gambling Museum (Las Vegas, Nevada)

Mobile Carnival Museum (Mobile, Alabama)

New England Pirate Museum (Salem, Massachusetts)

Ballard Institute and Museum of Puppetry (Mansfield, Connecticut)

National Cowgirl Museum and Hall of Fame (Fort Worth, Texas)

The Naughty Side of Museums

The Harry Mohney Erotic Museum, also known as the Erotic Heritage Museum, began as a collaboration between a Preacher (Reverend Ted McIlvenna) and a Pornographer (Harry Mohney). Inside is a collection of erotic artifacts, fine art, and film. Among the cooky and curious are the naughty museums that take a peek into the kinky and bizarre area of collectibles.

Museum of Sex (Manhattan, New York)

Leather Archives and Museum (Chicago, Illinois)

World Erotic Art Museum (Miami Beach, Florida)

Burlesque Hall of Fame (Las Vegas, Nevada)

Antique Vibrator Museum (San Francisco, California)

Museum of Historic Torture Devices (Wisconsin Dells, Wisconsin)

Field of Medical Museums

Though there are a variety of medical museums that detail the history of medicine, take a look at these museums that focus on a specific area. The Don & June Salvatori California Pharmacy Museum houses items that date back two centuries. The Pierre Fauchard Museum of Dental History is located on the Charleston Campus of the College of Southern Nevada. It is named for the father of modern dentistry.

Mutter Museum (Philadelphia, Pennsylvania)

Arkansas Country Doctor Museum (Lincoln, Arkansas)

History of Pharmacy Museum (University of Arizona)

Glore Psychiatric Museum (St. Joseph, Missouri)

The National Museum of Health and Medicine (Silver Spring, Maryland)

Museum of Questionable Medical Devices (St. Paul, Minnesota)

SKELETONS: A Museum of Osteology (Oklahoma City, Oklahoma)

Food and Beverage Museums

There is a treasure trove of museums solely devoted to a favorite food or beverage. There is an International Banana Museum in Mecca, California, and the Dr. Pepper Museum in Waco, Texas. The Honey of a Museum in Ashippun, Wisconsin, is dedicated to bees, beekeepers, and the history of honey. The Seymour Community Museum promotes a collection of hamburger memorabilia. At the Ye Ole Carriage Shop, there is a collection of over 500 pieces of Coca-Cola memorabilia. Here are more museums dedicated to our favorite snacks and drinks.

Edwin Perkins was a Hastings, Nebraska resident when he created Kool-aid in 1927. Today the community has a Kool-aid museum dedicated to the man and his invention. It is housed inside the Hastings Museum. Take a look at these food and beverage museums!

Spam Museum (Austin, Minnesota)

Iowa Dairy Museum (Calmar, Iowa)

Idaho Potato Museum (Blackfoot, Idaho)

Wyandot Popcorn Museum (Marion, Ohio)

O'Betty's Hot Dog Museum (Athens, Ohio)

Rock and Roll McDonald's (Chicago, Illinois)

Indian River Citrus Museum (Vero Beach, Florida)

Blue Bunny Ice Cream Parlor and Museum (Le Mars, Iowa)

Pacific Coast Cranberry Research Foundation Museum

National Mustard Museum (Middleton, Wisconsin)

National Apple Museum (Biglerville, Pennsylvania)

Museums of Crime and Punishment

In the world of law enforcement, there are dedicated museums spread across the United States. A few noteworthy museums explore the side of law enforcement that is not as discussed today. Arizona has the Gangster Museum of America that is dedicated to the history of organized crime. Artifacts at the DEA Museum show the impact of drug addiction from the past to the present. These fall under the category of – "they have a museum for that?!"

Crime Museum (Washington, D.C.)

International Spy Museum (Washington, D.C.)

CIA Museum (Annapolis Junction, Maryland)

National Cryptologic Museum (Annapolis Junction, Maryland)

Alcatraz East Crime Museum (Pigeon Forge, Tennessee)

U.S. Marshals Service National Museum (Fort Smith, Arkansas)

Animal Museums

The Wendell Gilley Museum in Harbor, Maine, has a collection of wooden bird carvings. Downstairs at the Everett Roehl Marshfield Public Library is the Stierle Bird Collection. This is an exhibit representing over 400 birds, that includes 2,000 bird eggs. Animals are a beloved part of our world, and these museums pay homage to some of our favorites.

Iditarod Museum (Wasilla, Alaska)

The MOOseum (Montgomery, Alabama)

Whale Museum (Friday Harbor, Washington)

Appaloosa Museum (Moscow, Idaho)

The Feline Historical Museum (Alliance, Ohio)

The Bunny Museum (Pasadena, California)

Greyhound Hall of Fame (Abilene, Kansas)

Bailey Saddle Shop & Museum (Simla, Colorado)

National Bird Dog Museum (Grand Junction, Tennessee)

American Quarter Horse Hall of Fame and Museum

Mr. Ed's Elephant Museum (Orrtanna, Pennsylvania)

Flyaways Waterfowl Experience (Baraboo, Wisconsin)

American Kennel Club Museum of the Dog (Saint Louis, Missouri)

National Museum of the Morgan Horse (Middlebury, Vermont)

National Bighorn Sheep Interpretive Center (Dubois, Wyoming)

Tennessee Walking Horse National Museum (Wartrace, Tennessee)

Museums for Houseware and Hardware

Collectibles

The Bell County Museum houses an impressive collection of mustache cups. In the Victorian Era, they had mustache cups that prevented a user's mustache from getting dunked in their tea. The exhibition at the Bell County Museum was featured on the Travel Channel. Inside Grannie's Cookie Jars & Ice-Cream Parlor is a small museum of cookie jars. A collection of over 2,600 and growing! These museums are dedicated to those little treasures that fill up our homes.

Hammer Museum (Los Angeles, California)

Button Museum (Bishopville, South Carolina)

Lock Museum of America (Terryville, Connecticut)

Trenton Teapot Museum (Trenton, Tennessee)

Museum of Salt and Pepper Shakers (Gatlinburg, Tennessee)

Vintage Sewing Center and Museum (Tulsa, Oklahoma)

Lee Maxwell Washing Machine Museum (Hurrich, Colorado)

Historical Event Museums

Museums have shown items that are wacky, adorable, crazy, and even the impressive. However, these museums take a page out of history and reexamine a time or event that changed the world. Florence Indian Mound Museum in Florence, Alabama, showcases artifacts that go back 10,000 years. The Donora Smog Museum details what led up to the events in 1948 when the smog in Donora became saturated with fluorine and took the lives of 20 people.

Johnstown Flood Museum (Johnstown, Pennsylvania)

National Voting Rights Museum (Selma, Alabama)

Freedom Rides Museum (Montgomery, Alabama)

Liberty Bell Museum (Allentown, Pennsylvania)

9/11 Memorial & Museum (New York, New York)

Titanic World's Largest Museum Attraction (Pigeon Forge, Tennessee)

Ireland's Great Hunger Museum (Quinnipiac University in Hamden, Connecticut)

Museums of Dolls & Toys (big & small)

At the National Bobblehead Hall of Fame and Museum, collectors can view 10,000 bobbleheads.

The Winifred Museum has over 3000 Tonka toys on display.

There are extraordinary doll museums that stand out from the others. Northlandz, in Flemington, New Jersey, is described as the world's largest miniature wonderland. They bost 200 dolls and a 94-room dollhouse. The Mama Muriel's Doll Museum houses dolls from the mid-1800's – American Girl dolls. Sandi Holder's Doll Attic holds the only Barbie Museum in America. The Morgan Doll Museum includes a collection of doll buggies. Klown Doll Museum in Plainview, Nebraska, showcases an impressive array of 7,000 clown dolls. These are a few more museums that concentrate on toys and dolls.

World Kite Museum (Long Beach, Washington)

National Farm Toy Museum (Dyersville, Iowa)

Bread and Puppet Museum (Glover, Vermont)

Spinning Top & Yo-Yo Museum (Burlington, Wisconsin)

Holiday Museums

Most people have a favorite holiday, and some have built a collection around it. These museums have housed a world of holiday collectibles. Whether you are a holiday collector or simply want to enjoy the rich history of different holidays, you will enjoy these museums. The Anna Jarvis Birthplace Museum was created for the founder of the Mother's Day holiday.

The Americanism Center Museum is owned and operated by the National Flag Day Foundation. It includes military artifacts and local history displays. Visitors can also learn about the life of Bernard J. CiGrand, the founder of Flag Day.

The Gargoyle Manor - The Monster Museum in Claudville, Virginia, is a favorite for Halloween fans. The museum displays artifacts of monster memorabilia, both fiction and nonfiction.

The Aluminum Tree and Ornament Museum is the only ornament dedicated to the metal Christmas trees. The "pop up" museum can be found at the Transylvania Heritage Museum, in Brevard, North Carolina, during November and December.

Halloween Museum (Salem, Massachusetts)

Castle Halloween Museum (Altoona, Pennsylvania)

Santa Claus Museum & Village (Santa Claus, Indiana)

Leavenworth Nutcracker Museum (Leavenworth, Washington)

National Christmas Center (Paradise, Pennsylvania)

Mystical & Occult Museums

At the International Cryptozoology Museum, there are exhibits related to the search for animals whose existence has not yet been proven. Salem, Massachusetts, is home to the Salem Witch Village, Witch History Museum, Salem Witch Board Museum, and the Salem Witch Museum. These museums are not as bizarre as they are intriguing. They tell a story of what "can be" and let the visitor decide if they choose to believe.

Paranormal Museum (Asbury Park, New Jersey)

Warren's Occult Museum (Monroe, Connecticut)

Dragon Dreams Museum (Chatanooga, Tennessee)

International UFO Museum and Research Center (Roswell, New Mexico)

Dedicated Industry Museums

Many people start a collection based on their career choice or reflect a job they once held. The Presidential Culinary Museum displays memorabilia from White House chefs, an excellent place for chefs and collectors of cooking memorabilia. These museums explore the history of different jobs.

Walmart Museum (Bentonville, Arkansas)

Postal History Foundation (Tucson, Arizona)

Plumbing Museum (Watertown, Massachusetts)

Simpson Funeral Museum (Chatham, Virginia)

International Lineman's Museum (Shelby, North Carolina)

First National Bank Museum (Columbia, Pennsylvania)

Dunlap Coke Ovens Mining Museum and Park (Dunlap, Tennessee)

Historical Home Museums Collectors Can Tour

Many homes of war heroes and politicians have since been made into museums and historical sites. Now we can explore the homes of others that have been memorialized in honor of their work and successes.

A Christmas Story House and Museum: This is the house at 3159 W 11th Street, Cleveland, Ohio, featured in A Christmas Story that was lived in by Ralphie and his family.

American Gothic House: This Eldon, Iowa home is also known as the Dibble House. It served as the background house in Grant Wood's iconic painting, American Gothic.

Belle Boyd House: The home at 126 E. Race Street, in Martinsburg, West Virginia, was the childhood home of Civil War spy, Belle Boyd. She provided information to Stonewall Jackson about enemy activities. She was imprisoned twice before she was deported back to England.

Booker T Washington House: He was born into slavery and rose to establish the Tuskegee Normal and Industrial Institute (now the Tuskegee University) in 1881 and the National Negro Business League two decades later.

Buffalo Bill Cody Homestead: Bill Cody served in the Civil War. He earned his nickname after he killed over 4,000 buffalo. He is remembered for his traveling Wild West show.

Carrie Chapman Catt Girlhood Home: As a Suffragette, Catt was instrumental in helping women to achieve the right to vote. History collectors can tour her childhood home at 2379 Timber Avenue, in Charles City, Iowa.

Dexter Parsonage Museum: This is the home where Martin Luther King, Jr. lived while preaching at the Dexter Avenue Church during the Montgomery Bus Boycott. King's family occupied the house at 315 S. Jackson Street, Montgomery, Alabama, from 1954-1960.

Dr. Bob's Home: The home at 855 Ardmore Avenue, Akron, Ohio, was the residency of Dr. Bob Smith and his wife, Anne. He is the co-founder of Alcoholic's Anonymous.

Dr. Samuel A. Mudd House: Dr. Mudd was an American physician accused of conspiring with John Wilkes Booth. His name has since become synonymous with disgracing yourself, as in the expression, "Your name is Mud!" The home at 3725 Dr. Samuel Mudd Road, Waldorf, Maryland, is filled with artifacts that were owned by the Mudd family.

Elmshaven: The home at 125 Glass Mountain Lane, Napa Valley, California, was once the residence of Ellen G. White. She is the founder of the Sabbatarian Adventist movement that led to Seventh-day Adventist Church.

Ferry Farm: This is the boyhood home of George Washington.

First White House of the Confederacy: This was the executive home of President Jefferson Davis and his family while the capital of the Confederate States of America was in Montgomery, Alabama. Many of their personal items are still in this home at 644 Washington Street, Montgomery, Alabama.

Harriet Tubman Home: The African Methodist Episcopal Zion Church owns and operates the former home of Harriet Tubman at 180 S Street Road, in Auburn, New York. It includes the Harriet Tubman Home for the Aged, the nearby Harriet Tubman Residence, and the Thompson A.M.E. Zion Church.

Ivy Green: This is the birthplace of Helen Keller. It was built in 1820 by her grandparents, David, and Mary Fairfax Moore Keller. The home at 300 North Commons Street West, Tuscumbia, Alabama, contains

Helen Keller's personal mementos. There is also memorabilia from the 25 countries where she gave lectures.

J.C. Penney House: This was the home of James Cash Penney, the founder of the J. C. Penney department stores. Today, the home at 722 J C Penney Drive, Kemmerer, Wyoming, tells the story of Penney's life.

Jennie Wade House: This was the home of the only resident killed during the Battle of Gettysburg. Jennie Wade was at home, in her kitchen, kneading dough, when a rifle bullet pierced two doors and claimed her life. She was only 20 years old.

Jesse James Farm and Museum: At 21216 Jesse James Farm Road, Kearney, Missouri, visitors can tour the cabin where Jesse James was born. They can also walk through the home that he was in with his brother, Frank, and their mother.

Johnny Cash Boyhood Home: Johnny Cash was three-years-old when his family moved into the home at 110 Denter Drive, Dyess, Arizona. He was five-years-old when he started working in his father's cotton fields. The family would sing songs while they worked.

Juliette Gordon Low Birthplace: She was the founder of the Girl Scouts of America. It is now the largest organization for girls in the world.

Leffingwell House Museum: The home at 348 Washington Street, Norwich, Connecticut, belonged to Christopher Leffingwell. This was a meeting place for soldiers during the Revolutionary War.

Nathan Hale Homestead Museum: Nathan Hale was a soldier in the Revolutionary War and a spy for the Continental Army. He was a hero to the country and especially to his home town. Today history buffs can visit his home in 2299 South Street in Coventry, Connecticut, that Nathan's father built.

Sequoyah's Cabin: This was the home of Sequoyah, also known as George Gist. He created a written language for the Cherokee Nation.

Stepping Stones: The home of Bill Wilson House. He is the co-founder of Alcoholic's Anonymous.

Sun Studio: In the music world, Sun Studio is the birthplace of Rock & Roll. Many music legends of yesterday were first recorded inside the walls of Sun Studio. Those musicians include Elvis Presley, Johnny Cash, Carl Perkins, Roy Orbison, and Jerry Lee Lewis.

The Witch House: This was the home of Judge Jonathan Corwin. He was the local magistrate during the Witchcraft Trials of 1692. It was his role to investigate the accusations that certain residents were witches. The house at 310 1/2 Essex Street, in Salem, Massachusetts, is the only structure left standing today that is connected to the trials, also known as the Corwin Witch Hunt.

Wyatt Earp Birthplace: was born on March 19, 1848, in the front bedroom of this modest home at 406 3rd Street in Monmouth, Illinois.

Tip 108: Visit Historical Sites to Expand Collectible Knowledge

Dinosaur Ridge: In Morrison, Colorado, are hundreds of footprints that were left fossilized in the ground. The tracks were left behind by duck-billed herbivores and ostrich-like carnivorous dinosaurs that roamed the area 150 million years ago. Today the site also includes dinosaur statues in memory of the ones that once called the area home.

Eli Whitney Museum: This is the site of the first factory built in America in 1798. He is best known for his invention of the cotton gin.

George Washington's Office: In downtown Winchester, at the corner of, sits the building that was once the office of George Washington. When Washington used it, from September 1755 to December of 1756, it was a small log structure, which today is the center part of the museum.

Meteor Crater: The exact spot where a meteor crashed into Arizona, 50,000 years ago. This is also known as Barringer Crater.

Rickwood Field was built in 1910 for the Birmingham Barons and the Birmingham Black Barons of the Negro Leagues. Today it is the oldest surviving professional baseball park in the United States.

Smokey Bear Historical Park: This is the site where the real Smokey Bear was rescued from a forest fire in 1950. He was treated for burns to his paws and hind legs. When he was well enough, he was relocated to the National Zoo in Washington, D.C., where he lived for the remainder of his life. When he died in 1976, he was sent back to New Mexico and buried at the park that bears his name – the Smokey Bear Historical Park.

Tip 109: Meet and Join Peer Groups for Collectors

There are two things that collectors enjoy: finding pieces for their collections and swapping stories about their treasures. Many have gone on to start clubs to meet fellow collectors. These are just some of the collector clubs in the world today!

American Bell Association International: Members are passionate about the organization, education, and collecting all types of bells.

American Breweriana Association: They are for historians and collectors of brewery and breweriana memorabilia.

American Hatpin Society: The members are dedicated to collecting and preserving hatpins and hatpin holders.

American Numismatic Association: This is a group dedicated to educating and encouraging people to collect coins.

Antique Fan Collectors Association: There are over 700 members who collect electrical and mechanical fans.

Antique Motorcycle Club of America: With over 11,000 members, they are the largest organization for antique motorcycle enthusiasts in the world.

Antique Truck Club of America: This is for people who own or are interested in antique commercial vehicles.

Brewery Collectibles Club of America: Members are collectors of alcohol and bar related items. That is also known as "breweriana."

Case Collectors Club: They were established for knife enthusiasts and collectors around the world.

Cookie Cutters Collectors Club: In 1971, Phyllis Wetherill wrote a letter to Woman's Circle Magazine searching for anyone who was collecting cookie cutters. She received four responses. This was the start of their club.

Florida Antique Tackle Collectors: They are dedicated to the education and preservation of angling history.

International Banana Club: This adorable club of banana collectors got its start in 1972. Today they have over 35,000 members from 27 countries.

International Coleman Collectors Club: Members of this club are interested in collecting, preserving, and restoring vintage Coleman products.

International Perfume Bottle Association: They are collectors of perfume bottles. They also have a virtual museum that explores the history of perfume bottles and vanity items.

Midwest Miniature Bottle Collectors: These club members have banded together to share a hobby of collecting miniature liquor bottles.

Musical Box Society: They are a group for collectors of music boxes and automatic musical instruments.

National American Glass Club: For glass collectors and all others concerned with the study and appreciation of glass, regardless of type, period, and origin.

National Association of Miniature Enthusiasts: The group promotes miniatures through education, collecting, and building friendships.

National Toothpick Holders Society: They have over 400 collectors of toothpick holders.

Novelty Salt and Pepper Shakers Collectors Club: This club has over 650 members from around the world, all with one common interest – the history and collecting of novelty and figural salt and pepper shakers.

Paperweight Collectors Association Inc: They are a group that is dedicated to appreciating and collecting glass paperweights.

Pepsi-Cola Collectors Club: The club was established for enthusiasts and collectors of all-things Pepsi.

Sorry Charlie No-Fan-Club-For-You Club: Collectors of Charlie, the Starkist mascot, reached out to the company to work with them in opening a club for the beloved character. However, the company was not interested. Cathy Runyan-Svacina decided to start the club itself and decided to give the club a name to spite Starkist's abrupt NO.

Statue of Liberty Club: Members are collectors and enthusiasts who want to preserve the statue's history.

Three Rivers Tool Collector's Association: Their members are collectors, sellers, users, and historians of all woodworking and metalworking tools of the past.

Transferware Collectors Club: This is for anyone who shares their passion for British Transferware made between 1760-1900.

UK Sucrologists Club – This is the first and only sugar packet collector's club.

About the Expert

Charlotte Hopkins is a freelance writer from Pittsburgh, Pennsylvania, who has been published in a variety of newspapers, magazines, and websites. She is the author of nine books, including her children's books, featuring Pixie Trist and Bo, and her "365 Days" series. She has been published in a variety of newspapers, magazines, and websites. She was also published three times in the Chicken Soup for the Soul series, the Shadows & Light Anthology, and Authors for Haiti. She is also a collector of several items. Her first collection was keychains, and today she collects penguins, wooden boxes, miniatures (including miniature books), Magic 8 Balls, journals, and wooden boxes. She just started another collection – pen cups! She has a fondness for writing, photography, astrology, history, museums, and everything purple.

HowExpert publishes quick 'how to' guides on all topics from A to Z by everyday experts. Visit HowExpert.com to learn more.

Recommended Resources

- HowExpert.com – Quick 'How To' Guides on All Topics from A to Z by Everyday Experts.
- HowExpert.com/free – Free HowExpert Email Newsletter.
- HowExpert.com/books – HowExpert Books
- HowExpert.com/courses – HowExpert Courses
- HowExpert.com/clothing – HowExpert Clothing
- HowExpert.com/membership – HowExpert Membership Site
- HowExpert.com/affiliates – HowExpert Affiliate Program
- HowExpert.com/writers – Write About Your #1 Passion/Knowledge/Expertise & Become a HowExpert Author.
- HowExpert.com/resources – Additional HowExpert Recommended Resources
- YouTube.com/HowExpert – Subscribe to HowExpert YouTube.
- Instagram.com/HowExpert – Follow HowExpert on Instagram.
- Facebook.com/HowExpert – Follow HowExpert on Facebook.